SANTA FE

A WALK THROUGH TIME

Staab and Galisteo Buildings, ca. 1933-34. (MNM # 51463)

NTA FE

A WALK THROUGH TIME

KINGSLEY HAMMETT

GIBBS P SMITH

West San Francisco Street, ca. 1918.
Photo by Wesley Bradfield.
(MNM # 14142)

This book is dedicated to all the wonderful citizens of Santa Fe.

First Edition
08 07 06 05 04   5 4 3 2 1

Text © 2004 **Kingsley Hammett**
Photographs © 2004 as noted throughout

Published by
Gibbs Smith, Publisher
P.O. Box 667
Layton, Utah 84041

Orders: 1.800.748.5439
www.gibbs-smith.com

Cover Photo: Don Gaspar Avenue, ca. 1935. Photo by T. Harmon Parkhurst. (MNM Neg. #11124)
Back Cover Photo: Interior, K.C. Waffle House, ca. 1935. Photo by T. Harmon Parkhurst. (MNM Neg. #50968)

Designed and produced by Peter Scholz
Jacket design by Steve Rachwal
Printed and bound in Korea

Library of Congress Cataloging-in-Publication Data
Hammett, Kingsley H.
  Santa Fe : a walk through time / Kingsley Hammett.
    p. cm.
  ISBN 1-58685-102-0
  1. Architecture—New Mexico—Santa Fe—Guidebooks. 2. Historic buildings—New Mexico—Santa Fe—Guidebooks.
3. Santa Fe (N.M.)—Buildings, structures, etc.—Guidebooks. 4. Santa Fe (N.M.)—Guidebooks. 5. Santa Fe (N.M.)—
History. I. Title.
NA735.S4334H35 2004
978.9'56—dc22
                              2004005055

Contents

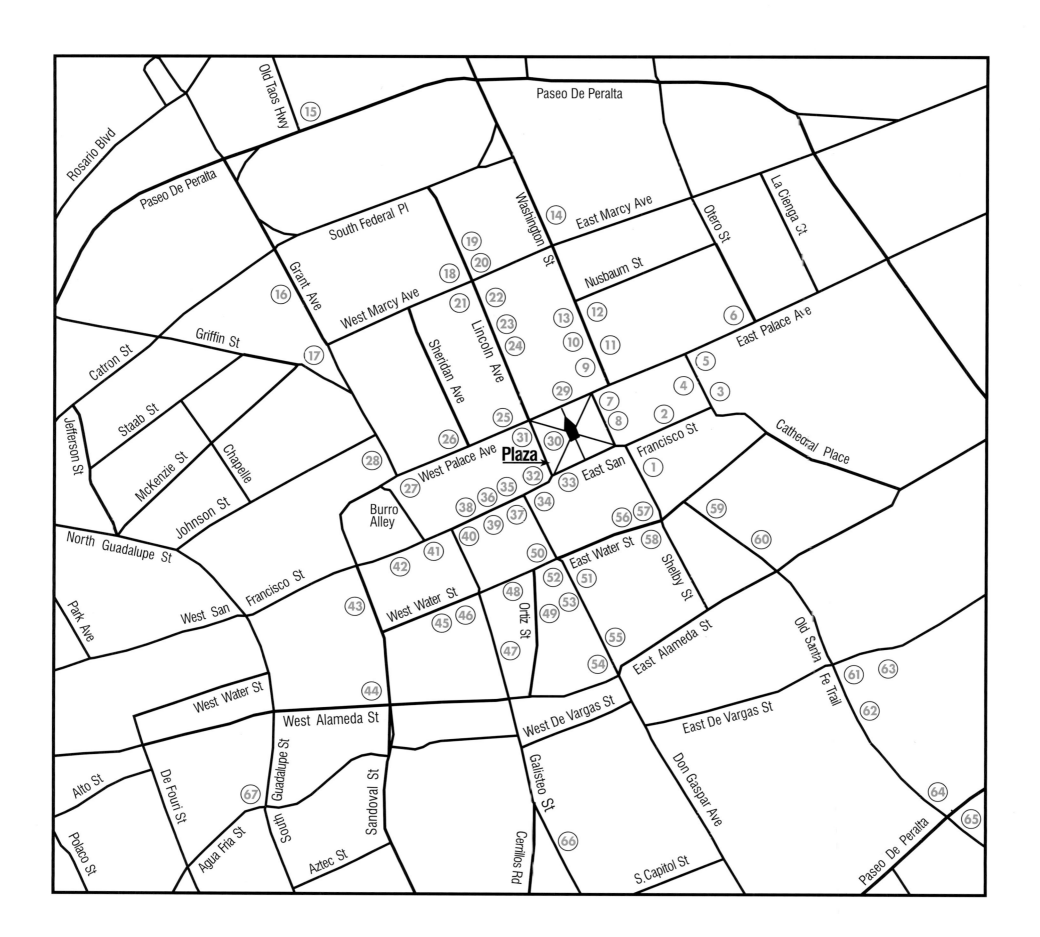

*El Oñate Theater
(Cassell Building), 1921.
(Detail of MNM # 10661)*

Acknowledgements

I want to acknowledge and thank the many Santa Feans who shared their recollections, which have been invaluable in filling in so many blanks on the map, including Samuel Adelo, Jane E. Arp, Deborah Auten, John Barker, Laughlin Barker, Fabian Chavez, Tom Closson, Mary Jean Cook, John Conron, Jim Downey, Michel Fidel, Alexis Greer, E. John Greer Jr., Connie Hernandez, James Hewat, Janice Matthews, Sara Melton, Marian Meyer, Robert Montoya, Theo Raven, Frances Rios, Socorro Rios, Teresa Rios, Bill Sauter, Paul Shaya, Mary Rios Smith, Cordelia Snow, Beverly Spears, and Valentin Valdez. Invaluable has been the assistance of Richard Rudisill and Arthur Olivas, former curators of the Fray Angelico Chavez Photographic Archives, whose vast collection and years of experience hold much of the collective memory of Santa Fe as captured in photographs. Thanks to Tomas Jaehn and Hazel Romero of the History Library at the Museum of New Mexico; and to Jo Anne Jager and Guadalupe Martinez at the New Mexico State Library, who led me to invaluable resources to sort out the facts behind conflicting stories that swirl around Santa Fe's past. Thanks also to Kathy Gavey and her fellow volunteers at the Menaul Historical Library for information regarding the activities of the Presbyterian Church, and to Carla Rodriguez of the Guadalupe Historic Foundation. I also want to thank Bonita Barlow for her artistic eye and contemporary photographs, Gillian Ashley for her skilled proofreading, and Jeffrey Horton for his informative map. And I want to close with a loving thank-you to my wife, partner, and editor, Jerilou Hammett, whose resourcefulness, organization, and sense of layout and design have brought this project out of chaos and into cohesion.

Preface

The Santa Fe that tourists come to see today bears little resemblance to the city of just a few decades ago. In those days, within a three-block radius of the Plaza, new generations of Santa Feans were born at St. Vincent Hospital at the corner of Palace Avenue and Paseo de Peralta. Santa Fe High School students attended classes on Lincoln Avenue and ate lunch in the park on the north side of South Federal Place, where the post office now stands. After school they'd flood the Plaza and buy a soda at Zook's Pharmacy. Housewives would shop for groceries at Batrite's, Piggly Wiggly, and Safeway, fill their prescriptions at Central and Capital pharmacies, buy clothes at J. C. Penney's, Bell's, and Goodman's, shoes at Pfluger's and Kahn's, and notions at Woolworth's and Taichert's. For fashions they went to The Guarantee, La Tienda, and El Pavon. Locals posted letters at the old post office opposite the cathedral, bought appliances at the Maytag shop, purchased furniture at Montoya's and Livingston's, found a plumber at Cartwright's, and got lumber and hardware at Big Jo's. Folks stood in line for a steak at the U and I, chop suey at the New Canton Cafe, or a burger at the Little Chief Grill Cafe. There was a gas station on almost every corner, a tire store on Lincoln Avenue, places to get your shoes repaired, and a choice of three movie theaters on West San Francisco Street. The Plaza was where you met old friends and paused to chat.

But that's all gone now. The Santa Fe that once served Santa Feans has become a destination serving tourists, loaded with shops few locals have interest in and most can't afford. Strict zoning laws have kept the downtown a conformist Pueblo-style brown, but exceptions have allowed new buildings to tower above the narrow streets, their mass blocking the views of distant mountains.

Lost in those changes is the memory of what once was. I used to patronize the Bank of Santa Fe, where the massive First Interstate Bank building now stands, and I have no recollection of what the old bank looked like. I ate in restaurants that have become boutiques. I filled my tank at gas stations where vendors now sell Central American imports. I bought shoelaces where art galleries now sit. Whole blocks of memory have been wiped from my mind. And I know I'm not alone. Even families who have been here for generations can't remember what once stood on a certain corner. So I decided it was time to reconstruct some of that lost memory before much more of Santa Fe is altered forever.

– K.H.H , Santa Fe, NM , 2004

Plaza, ca. 1912. Photo by Jesse L. Nusbaum. (Detail of MNM # 139151)

Introduction

The Spanish established Santa Fe as the capital of *El Norte* in 1610. It was laid out according to the Laws of the Indies, a set of town planning ordinances promulgated by King Philip II of Spain in 1573 that designated the location of church, government, and commercial buildings around a plaza. Along the north side of the Santa Fe Plaza, founder Don Pedro de Peralta located what would become known as the Palace of the Governors. To the east he placed the village church. During the city's first two hundred years Santa Fe had no need for a commercial district, so the other two sides of the Plaza were devoted to the houses of prominent citizens.

Out from the Plaza radiated a tight grid of streets, which within a few blocks gave way to a tangle of dirt paths that followed the natural and man-made watercourses and burro trails that wound around the hills to the east of downtown and west along the banks of the Santa Fe River. Farmers tended small plots of corn and chile and watered orchards of peaches, apples, and apricots. Few buildings other than churches stood more than one story high. All was built of rough adobe brick, plastered in mud and roofed with dirt. The occasional caravan of oxcarts ground its way north from Mexico along *El Camino Real* (a viable commercial route for 225 years before the Santa Fe Trail opened). Periodically soldiers set out to engage marauding bands of Comanches and Apaches. Otherwise,

life was a humble ritual of farm labor, barter, and religious ceremony.

Once Mexico broke free from Spain in 1821, it opened the New Mexican territory for trade with the eastern United States. Wagon trains from Missouri loaded with shiny tools and bright calico caused great anticipation as they rumbled over Glorieta Pass down what's now known as the Old Santa Fe Trail, and into the Santa Fe Plaza. Merchants began to erect larger buildings along the south side of the Plaza to serve as both retail stores and wholesale warehouses, and long-isolated Santa Feans encountered a whole new world.

In 1846, General Stephen Watts Kearny led a troop of cavalry into the city and claimed the entire New Mexican territory for the United States as a spoil of its war with Mexico. The army brought with it new tools and materials that created rapid change within a few short decades in this dusty provincial outpost. The military imported the region's first power saw, which produced dimensioned lumber and led to the Territorial style of architecture, marked by Greek revival pediments over doors and windows and square portal posts. Eastern and military influences inspired New England and Midwestern housing designs and details like pitched roofs, brick walls and roofline coping, picket fences, and multi-paned, factory-made windows.

For the next thirty years, trade over the Santa Fe Trail thrived as Missouri drovers brought everything and anything imaginable from Independence and points east, including brick, tin roof panels, plate glass, nails, store-bought clothes and shoes, and even pianos. German-Jewish sutlers, who came to supply the U.S. Army, stayed to service Santa Fe, the outlying farming villages, and the entire territory. Bishop (later Archbishop) Jean Baptiste Lamy arrived in 1851 with grand plans to improve the health, education, and welfare of his new flock. He left a legacy of churches, schools, hospitals, and social institutions, many built in styles then popular in his native France.

In 1880, an eighteen-mile railroad spur connected the capital city to the mainline of the Atchison, Topeka, and Santa Fe Railway. New supplies of more varied building materials transformed the large adobe commercial buildings around the Plaza into even larger Victorian ones. New brick buildings were embellished with popular architectural details like pressed tin ceilings, cast-iron columns, and factory-made window sashes and doors. But in an irony of history, the coming of the railroad, while initially cause for much celebration and optimism, ultimately sent the capital city into a spiral of economic decline. Overnight the Santa Fe Trail that had been so lucrative became obsolete as territorial commerce shifted from Santa Fe to the mainline depots of Las Vegas and Albuquerque. The city's civilian population also declined. And to make matters worse, the federal government closed Fort Marcy in the early 1890s, taking with it significant payroll and purchasing power.

By the early decades of the twentieth century, Santa Fe was in a state of architectural confusion. In an attempt to win Congressional approval for statehood, it tried to remake itself into Anywhere, USA, and largely succeeded. Guadalupe Church had changed its appearance from Northern New Mexico Mission to tall-steepled rural France. Politicians met in an imposing marble and granite capitol with a grand columned portico and rotunda beneath a stained-glass dome that rivaled the best in the nation. Visitors put up at the elaborate Palace Hotel, decorated with New Orleans–style iron columns, wraparound balconies, and filigree-topped towers. The shopping blocks were Victorian Italianate. Much new housing was Bungalow and California Mission style. The Catholic schools were French Second Empire. And St. Francis Cathedral and Loretto Chapel were Gothic and Romanesque Revival.

By the time New Mexico finally gained statehood in 1912, the city fathers had realized they needed to replace the lost commerce of the army and the Trail with a new economic engine and were seeking to establish Santa Fe as the center for tourism in the Southwest. They needed a theme, a cohesive appearance, a style that would attract visitors and distinguish the city from the Spanish Mission Revival then taking hold in California. They soon found it with the restoration of the Palace of the Governors and the construction of the Fine Arts Museum. Santa Fe would henceforth be known as the city of Spanish Pueblo Revival, some of its identify rooted in authenticity, much of it fabricated. The new tastemakers used as the basis for their emergent style the protruding vigas, overhanging canales, and carved corbels they found on the remnants of original Santa Fe adobe homes. Architects looked for inspiration among the Pueblo mission churches built centuries before. And they drew up an informal design code: all present and future buildings in historic Santa Fe should display a uniform, earth-toned, adobe look. They ripped off the cast-iron storefronts, tore down the gingerbread trim, took off the Victorian brackets and dentils, discarded the Grecian columns, and covered brick and stone facades with layers of brown cement. By the 1930s, this narrow definition of acceptable style had been broadened to allow buildings that embraced the details of the Territorial period, including sharper corners, brick roof coping, and square portal columns. It also allowed Greek Revival window and door pediments, all painted white.

Forcing existing buildings to conform yielded some alterations that were more successful than others. The remnants of these waves of change are still visible around the downtown, sometimes on the same building. The second Spiegelberg building, for example, on the south side of the Plaza (now known as Simply Santa Fe), still has an entry framed in Victorian cast iron imported from Pittsburgh, covered by a Spanish Pueblo Revival portal, and topped by Territorial-style brick coping.

In the mad rush to "pueblofy" Santa Fe, the city lost a great deal of its architectural history and eclectic charm. By the early 1950s, John Conron's Centerline Building, featuring a California stick style, sent shivers of fear through the traditionalists, who then prompted the city to adopt the Historic Styles Ordinance to codify the agreed-upon look and to police any violations thereof.

Santa Fe is still The City Different, still a charming place, and to most visitors it looks nothing like where they come from. While the charms survive despite a history of massive changes, in recent years a once vibrant and living city center has been tamed into an adobe theme park. The alterations have left an incomplete but fascinating trail, in the form of photographs and insurance maps, newspaper clippings and business directory listings. Come now on a historical walking tour, take a look into the past, and recall some of what has been lost.

1. Exchange Hotel/La Fonda

East San Francisco Street at Old Santa Fe Trail

A hostelry, known by a succession of names, has sat across from the southeast corner of the Plaza at the end of the Santa Fe Trail for as long as anyone can remember. Travelers in 1849 describe dining well and finding "comfortable drink" at the United States (or U.S.) Hotel. By 1871, *The Santa Fe New Mexican* newspaper described recent improvements to what was then called the Exchange Hotel. It was now "unquestionably one of the most commodious and comfortable hotels in the West" with the best management this side of the Mississippi. An 1886 insurance map identified the same establishment as the Capital Hotel and made no secret of its gambling room, which appeared prominently on the map.

By 1890 it was once again called the Exchange Hotel. But by the turn of the century it was in steep decline and the front rooms were occupied by the Kinsell Livestock Co. Meat Market.

In 1919, the building was demolished and replaced by a new hotel named La Fonda, the last major project of Isaac Hamilton Rapp, the Colorado architect who has become known as the father of Santa Fe style. Local businessmen launched the project by securing pledges of almost $200,000 for its construction. Six years after opening, the hotel was taken over by the Fred Harvey Company, the fabled hospitality organization that owned hotels and restaurants all along the Atchison, Topeka, and Santa Fe railroad line.

Old Exchange Hotel building. (MNM #13040)

Exchange Hotel, ca. 1880. (MNM #38368)

The takeover prompted the *New Mexican* to excitedly announce that La Fonda would finally be providing "Harvey hotel service, Harvey hotel food, Harvey hotel standards."

By 1929, La Fonda underwent a major interior redesign by Mary Colter (Harvey's company architect who created and decorated many of his buildings, including those at the Grand Canyon), and an extensive exterior renovation and addition by local architect John Gaw Meem. Meem came to Santa Fe in the early 1920s to recuperate from tuberculosis and became a volunteer for the Society for the Restoration and Preservation of New Mexico Missions, one of which was the church at Acoma Pueblo, the group's longest and most costly undertaking.

In the project at La Fonda, Meem added considerably to the hotel's capacity and put a six-story bell tower, reminiscent of the towers he was in the process of restoring at Acoma, at the building's southwest corner. For the next forty years Meem enjoyed a distinguished career designing many of Santa Fe's major landmark buildings and helping to popularizing both the Spanish Pueblo and Territorial Revival styles.

For the next fifty years, La Fonda served as the center of Santa Fe's social swirl, where buses brought visitors to and from the railroad depot in Lamy; where journalists hung out to buttonhole celebrities for a quick interview; where local swells danced the *varsoviana* in the New Mexican Room; and where memorable Fiesta parties rocked the bar and filled the roof with revelers. In 1948, Mary Colter reorganized the San Francisco Street façade and converted what had been an open patio into street-front shops. A parking garage and more rooms were added in the 1980s and '90s. Today the hotel has 160 rooms and remains a beacon for travelers in search of a bit of Santa Fe nostalgia.

Kinsell Livestock Co. Meat Market, ca. 1900–1905. (MNM #105576)

La Fonda Hotel. Photo by T. Harmon Parkhurst. (MNM #10692)

2. St. Francis Parochial School

122 East San Francisco Street

Bishop (later Archbishop) Jean Baptiste Lamy arrived in Santa Fe in the summer of 1851. The next year he went back east to escort four Sisters of Loretto to Santa Fe over the Santa Fe Trail. The party arrived in Santa Fe in September 1852, and the following January the sisters founded New Mexico's first school for girls, in an adobe building opposite La Parroquia (see page 22). In the following decades, their Loretto Academy became an important local institution for the secondary education of young women (see pages 142 and 144).

Sometime after the turn of the twentieth century, the sisters built the brick building (shown here) across the street from St. Francis Cathedral, where they operated their St. Francis Parochial School for boys and girls. They remained in this location until 1950, when they moved into the new St. Francis Cathedral School at the corner of Paseo de Peralta and East Alameda Street. The original school building was then razed to make way for a parking lot for La Fonda hotel. In 1985, the hotel built an enclosed garage on that site. The hotel enlarged the structure in 1997 to include a rooftop bar and additional second-story suites.

St. Francis School, ca. 1914.
(MNM #50904)

3. La Parroquia/St. Francis Cathedral

131 Cathedral Place

Fray Alonso de Benavides built the city's first real church on this site in about 1626. It stood at the east end of what then was probably a much larger Plaza as dictated by the Laws of the Indies. The church was destroyed in the Pueblo Revolt of 1680, and by 1712 it had been replaced by a large adobe building called La Parroquia ("the parish church"), whose crenellated walls and twin towers echoed those of a Moorish castle.

It served as the city's primary church until 1869, when Bishop Lamy helped lay the cornerstone (stolen the next day and never seen again!) for a formal Romanesque Revival cathedral modeled on the one then under construction in Marseilles in his native France. He brought to Santa Fe French architects and Italian stonemasons, who built the present cathedral over and around La Parroquia with sandstone from his own private quarry near the present town of Lamy.

Many of his friends in the local German-Jewish merchant community donated significant sums to the cathedral's completion. Over its main entrance is a triangle, which the bishop had carved into the stone, inscribed with the four letters of the ancient Hebrew name for God. Whether this was a sign of gratitude for the gifts from his Jewish friends or simply a common Christian symbol remains unclear.

When the cathedral was finished in 1884, workers tore down the adobe walls of La Parroquia, carried the bricks out the door, and used them to smooth the ruts in nearby streets.

La Parroquia, ca. 1868.
(MNM #10059)

St. Francis Cathedral under construction, ca. 1880. Photo by B. H. Gurnsey. (MNM #131794)

St. Francis Cathedral, ca. 1913. Photo by Jesse L. Nusbaum. (Detail of MNM # 61350)

4. Cathedral Convent/Old Federal Post Office

108 Cathedral Place

Old convent, ca. 1919. Photo by Carter H. Harrison. (MNM #10093)

The Sisters of Loretto came to Santa Fe in 1852 to establish New Mexico's first school for girls, and in January 1853 thirteen students held their first classes in this low adobe building across from La Parroquia. Six months later enrollment was up to forty-two students. Within a few years the sisters moved their school into La Casa Americana, originally a hotel, before building their own convent on the site in the 1890s (see pages 144-145). The row of adobe rooms briefly quartered Confederate troops just after the Civil War battle at Glorieta. By 1919 it was torn down

to make room for a new federal building and post office, which opened in 1922. The plaque on the northeast corner of that building identifies the designer as a federal employee, presumably out of Washington, D.C., who had a distinct sense of the Spanish Pueblo Revival style then taking root in Santa Fe. After a new post office went up just west of the federal courthouse on South Federal Place in the early 1960s, this building was given over to other governmental uses, including offices for the Internal Revenue Service. Today it is home to the Institute of American Indian Arts Museum.

U.S. Post Office and federal building, ca. 1925–30. (MNM #56431)

5. St. Vincent Sanatorium

Cathedral Place

Sister Vincent O'Keefe and three other Sisters of Charity came out from Cincinnati in 1865 and established St. Vincent Hospital and Orphanage in an old adobe building just north of La Parroquia. In 1878, Archbishop Lamy began overseeing construction of a large Second Empire-style structure on Cathedral property. He'd hoped it would serve as a vocational school. But by then the sisters had far outgrown their old hospital, so the new building, now the tallest in the city, opened instead in 1883 as St. Vincent Sanatorium. It had patients' dining rooms and parlors on the first floor, dormitories and a patients' ward on the second, and on the third were a chapel and hall with a large stage that became a sort of community center for raffles, bands, and classes in music, painting, and drawing.

Thirteen years later the Sanatorium burned to the ground. It was replaced in 1910 by Marian Hall, a new seventy-five bed hospital located further east on Palace Avenue, which a 1920 promotional brochure for health seekers described as "the most delightful nook in the Rocky Mountains." Sanatorium charges for private patient rooms and suites ran from $100 to $160 per month. Guests of patients could stay overnight for $3. Once the new 211-bed, four-story St. Vincent Hospital opened next door at the corner of Palace Avenue and Paseo de Peralta in 1953, Marian Hall's first two floors were remodeled into a convent and the third into nurses' quarters. After the current St. Vincent Hospital was built south of town on St. Michael's Drive in 1977, the 1953 hospital and Marian Hall became state offices and a nursing home. The old hospital building is now in private hands awaiting redevelopment.

Today, beyond the 130-year-old sandstone pillars that framed the entrance drive to the Sanatorium is the recently renovated Cathedral Park, home to occasional weekend art shows, a new sculpture honoring the early Spanish settlers, and benches that offer a shady resting spot for weary tourists.

St. Vincent Industrial School,
Sanatorium, Hospital, built 1880,
burned July 1896.
(Detail of MNM #67743)

6. Santa Fe County Courthouse/Coronado Building

141 East Palace Avenue

Santa Fe County Courthouse, ca. 1888. Photo by W. E. Hook. (Detail of MNM #56044)

Santa Fe County Courthouse, ca. 1920.
Photo by Aaron B. Craycroft.
(MNM #10233)

According to the insurance map of 1886, the area across Palace Avenue from St. Vincent Sanatorium was the location of the city's ice-skating rink. A few years later, Santa Fe County built a magnificent brick Victorian courthouse with sandstone quoins on the site.

Fire gutted that building on February 8, 1909, and in its place the county built a stolid modified-Greek Revival building with imposing Ionic columns designed by Isaac Hamilton Rapp and his brother William, who constituted one of Santa Fe's earliest and most favored architectural firms and who left an indelible stamp on the city in a variety of styles.

The Works Progress Administration (WPA) funded a new county courthouse designed by John Gaw Meem in the Spanish Pueblo Revival style on Grant Avenue at the corner of Johnson Street in 1939 (see page 77). The original courthouse building then moved into private hands, got a Territorial facelift from architect Gordon Street, and was ultimately renamed the Coronado Building. For years it housed various doctors' offices, located as it was directly across the street from the hospital. Today it is home to a number of law and financial firms. When the current tenants on the second floor renovated the space and removed an old false ceiling, they found the original coffered ceiling and plaster trim from the early decades of the twentieth century, when it was a courtroom presided over by Judge Miguel Antonio Otero Jr.

Coronado Building, ca. 1950. (MNM #55019)

7. Johnson Building/Catron Block

53–55 Old Santa Fe Trail

When the Johnson Building sat at the northeast corner of the Plaza in the 1870s, *The Santa Fe New Mexican* operated out of a space on the Palace Avenue side, and the First National Bank occupied rooms facing the Plaza under the portal. On the second floor were the offices of attorney Thomas B. Catron, leader of the notorious Santa Fe Ring, a group of powerful ranchers, businessmen, and politicians that controlled virtually the entire New Mexican economic and political landscape in the Territorial period.

In 1891, Catron replaced the Johnson Building with a fine $40,000 Italianate structure that bore his name (the Catron Block). He hoped it would eventually include a second-floor opera house. The company that built the Catron Block was operated by members of two Italian stonemason families – Palladino and Berardinelli – whom Archbishop Lamy had brought to Santa Fe to complete the Cathedral. They used brick manufactured at the state penitentiary (then located about a mile south of the Plaza) and decorated the façade with a pressed-metal cornice shipped out from the East. In 1912, Emil and Johanna Uhfelder opened the White House, the city's first women's fashions store, on the ground floor.

When their daughter Pauline married Barnett Petchesky in 1922, the young couple opened The Guarantee shoe store next to the White House. The family bought the building from Catron's heirs in 1927 and in succeeding decades sublet some of the ground-floor space

Johnson Block (Santa Fe Finishing School and U.S. Post Office), ca. 1880. (MNM #10713)

Catron Block. Photo by E. V. Harris. (MNM #67593)

to a number of department stores, including Hinkel's, Hubbard's, and Dunlap's. Shortly after World War II, the separate shoe and women's ready-to-wear stores were combined under the name The Guarantee and expanded into additional space fronting Palace Avenue formerly occupied by the Cash and Carry grocery store. A decade later Pauline's son Gene Petchesky (and his wife Jane) and daughter Marian (and her husband Abe Silver) took over the store. They added a Territorial-style *portal* in the late 1960s. Ten years later the details of the lower story were hidden behind cement stucco, and the original large display windows were replaced by smaller ones to conform to Santa Fe style. In the mid-1980s, the author built a Spanish Pueblo Revival style *portal* over the Palace Avenue entrance. But the original ornate Victorian detailing is still clearly visible along the second story of the Catron Block where eyebrow lintels over the windows and an elaborate roof cornice make this the last remaining example of the Victorian architecture that once dominated the Plaza area.

Catron Block, 2003. Photo by Bonita Barlow.

First National Bank. (MNM #10640)

8. First National Bank/Eagle Dancer

57 Old Santa Fe Trail

The Rapp brothers designed this exquisite example of Greek Revival architecture in 1912. It was the last building to go up on the Plaza before the city fathers decided to make Santa Fe the center of Southwest tourism and forced every building to conform to the new Santa Fe style. That led to the remodeling of most of the downtown buildings into either the Spanish Pueblo Revival or Territorial Revival styles and to the removal of all references to traditional American architecture. John Gaw Meem designed a retrofit for this building in 1957, which was then occupied by Levine's Department Store. The classic façade was to be removed and the second story sheathed in plate glass shaded by a cornice supported by a row of carved corbels. But the remodel was never fully realized, and in the end the front wound up plastered in brown cement stucco above a Spanish Pueblo Revival *portal*. Now the building is home to the Eagle Dancer gift shop, yet it retains some interior elements of the original bank, most notably its massive safe. The First National Bank itself moved across the Plaza in the mid-1950s to occupy a building originally designed in the 1920s as a movie theater (see page 85).

Eagle Dancer, 2003. Photo by Bonita Barlow.

9. National Guard Armory/Hall of Ethnology

110 Washington Avenue

The National Guard built this grand armory just north of the Palace of the Governors in 1909 to replace an older facility on Water Street. By late 1939, after another armory had been built south of town on Old Pecos Trail, John Gaw Meem drew up plans to remodel the Washington Avenue armory in the new Santa Fe style by building a room onto the front and hiding the original fortress-like details under a coat of brown cement plaster. The next June, local WPA officials received the welcome news that President Franklin D. Roosevelt had authorized $12,665 to get the project rolling. The remodeled structure became part of the Palace of the Governors and eventually housed the State History Library and Photographic Archives. Today it is a place for exhibitions and meetings, with offices upstairs for museum officials. But a large, three-story addition planned for the rear and sides of the Palace of the Governors will soon replace most of this building, although the Meem façade will be preserved.

National Guard Armory, 1909.
Photo by Jesse L. Nusbaum. (MNM #61399)

Hall of Ethnology, Museum of New Mexico. (MNM #6754)

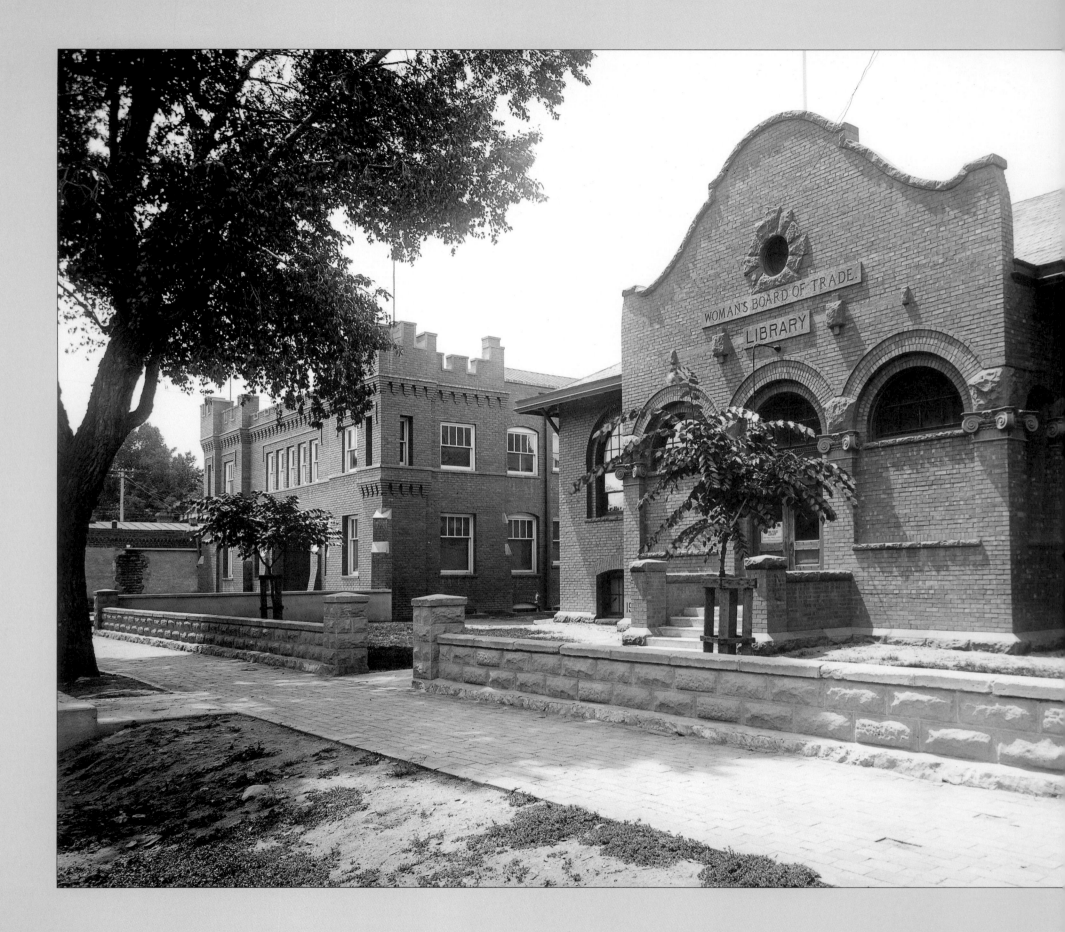

10. Women's Board of Trade Library/ Fray Angelico Chavez History Library and Photographic Archives

120 Washington Avenue

The Women's Board of Trade organized the city's first library in 1892 and gave it a real home in 1907 in this Mission Revival building. It got a John Gaw Meem-designed Territorial facelift in 1932, and the next year he arranged through the WPA to have artist Olive Rush paint a charming mural in the foyer (still there today) with the reminder (in Spanish) that "With good books you are not alone." The City of Santa Fe acquired the building in 1961 and continued to support it as a public library until 1987. The library then moved across and up the street into the refurbished Meem-designed Berardinelli Building, which earlier had housed the city's offices, jail, and police and fire stations. A human chain of volunteers stretched across Washington Avenue and passed armloads of books one to another to move the library to its new home. The old library building then passed into the hands of the state and was remodeled for use as the Fray Angelico Chavez History Library and Photographic Archives.

Women's Board of Trade Library, ca. 1912.
Photo by Jesse L. Nusbaum.
(Detail of MNM # 56603)

11. State Securities Building/Anasazi Hotel

113 Washington Avenue

For decades the State Securities Building housed several governmental bureaus, including the central offices of the State Corrections Department and a juvenile detention center. In 1991, interior designer Bob Zimmer, along with Japanese investors, bought it with plans to convert it into the small luxury Anasazi Hotel. To exorcise any negative energy that might still be lurking from the days when its former tenants ruled over the state's penitentiary population, Zimmer stripped it down to its bare steel skeleton and had what remained blessed by holy men of every description. He then rebuilt it in the Spanish Pueblo Revival style with extraordinary craftsmanship and attention to detail, incorporating interior features – particularly stonework – that is reminiscent of the Native American ruins at Chaco Canyon.

State Securities Building, ca. 1976-77. Photo by Arthur Taylor. (MNM # 117159)

Anasazi Hotel, 2003. Photo by Bonita Barlow.

12. Nusbaum House

125 Washington Avenue

This single-story, Territorial-style house with its broad front veranda was originally owned by Dr. Henry Connelly, a Kentuckian who married into the local culture. He established trading posts in Santa Fe, Albuquerque, and Peralta and served as Territorial governor during the Civil War. He sold the house to Lehman Spiegelberg, a member of a large German-Jewish merchant clan, in 1874 for $3,500. It was here the Spiegelberg family entertained President Rutherford B. Hayes in 1880. They remained in the home until moving to New York in 1891.

In 1906, Lehman's wife, Carrie L. Spiegelberg, sold the home to Levi A. Hughes, who resold it a month later to Dora R. Nusbaum. Dora's husband Simon died in 1921, but she remained in residence, added a second story in the 1940s, and took in boarders until moving out herself in 1958. The building was torn down in 1960 in one of two perceived architectural crimes (the construction of the Centerline Building being the other; see pages 56-57) that spurred the creation of the Historic Santa Fe Foundation and the movement to preserve Santa Fe's architectural legacy. For thirty years the city leased the land for a municipal parking lot. In 1990, the Territorial-style Hotel Plaza Real was built on the site.

Simon and Dora Nusbaum residence (formerly Spiegelberg residence). (MNM # 61487)

Nusbaum House, July 1960. Photo by Tyler Dingee. (MNM # 91901)

13. Otero House/Santa Fe National Bank/ First Interstate Building

150 Washington Avenue

With the U.S. occupation of New Mexico in 1846, a garrison of federal troops took over almost seventeen acres of downtown Santa Fe north and west of the Palace of the Governors and built Fort Marcy. Houses like this one, used by army officers, lined much of Washington, Lincoln, and Grant Avenues. This house, first occupied by the fort's commanding officer, later served as the home of Territorial Governor Miguel Otero.

For a period of years after 1915 it served as the Santa Fe Club, and it is remembered as the scene of many scandalous parties. Then between 1921 and 1929, according to insurance maps, the building was the Knights of Columbus Home. For the next three years it was the Sayre Funeral Home, and for a year or so in the late '30s it was the Republican State Headquarters. On September 9, 1946, *The Santa Fe New Mexican* announced the grand opening of the Santa Fe National Bank on this site – one of the first large public structures to be built in the post-war era – complete with a drive-up window and parking lot.

In the early 1980s, most of this end of the block was cleared through to Lincoln Avenue and the four-story First Interstate Building rose on the site. As one of the city's first massive commercial projects, it declared to Santa Feans that the end of the traditional low-slung profile of the City Different had come.

Commanding officer's quarters (later M. A. Otero residence), Fort Marcy. (MNM #1695)

*Santa Fe National Bank,
ca. 1976-77.
Photo by Arthur Taylor.
(Detail of MNM # 117182)*

First Interstate Building, 2003. Photo by Bonita Barlow.

14. Palace Hotel

Washington Avenue near Marcy Avenue

Once the Atchison, Topeka, and Santa Fe Railway laid an eighteen-mile spur from the mainline station in Lamy to Santa Fe in 1880, the capital city needed a proper hotel. The answer was the elaborate Italianate Palace Hotel built of clapboard with a mansard roof and wrought-iron detailing. The hotel opened in October 1881 on Washington Avenue opposite the Fort Marcy parade grounds on the corner of what today is Marcy Avenue.

A drawing dated November 1, 1912, in the period when Santa Fe was flush with the excitement of statehood, shows an architect's idea of how to turn this Victorian jewel into ersatz Spanish Pueblo Revival and bring it aboard the Santa Fe-style bandwagon then building speed. Three years later it had been renamed the Hotel DeVargas, and a railroad postcard advised travelers headed to San Diego's Panama-California Exposition, "When you get your ticket to the Pacific Coast Exhibition in 1915, be sure to arrange

for the free side trip to Santa Fe. Put up at the Hotel DeVargas, the only first-class hotel in the city." Seven years later, on January 4, 1922, a ferocious blaze reduced the entire structure to a pile of ashes except for a single, naked three-story chimney.

According to an insurance map, the site was still empty in 1931. But by 1942 it was occupied by a corner filling station and Miller Motors, Inc., dealers in Lincoln and Mercury cars. Miller Motors was later replaced by Miles Motors, Santa Fe's Chrysler/Plymouth dealership, which held its grand opening in 1949.

But Miles Motors was gone from this location after 1953, and the showroom building was next occupied by the New Mexico Department of Public Welfare and other state and private offices. Today it is a mix of retail shops and offices, while the filling station, long known as Bennie's Gulf, hung on into the 1980s to become one of downtown's last places to buy gas. It was then remodeled into a branch office of First State Bank.

Palace Hotel, ca. 1890. (MNM # 10766)

*Drawing of remodeling plan
for Palace Hotel in "Santa Fe"
style, November 1, 1912.
(MNM # 61426)*

Sage Memorial Building, Allison-James School. (Menaul Historical Library, Photo Album Access # 1995.164)

15. Allison-James School

Paseo de Peralta at Old Taos Highway

Throughout most of the twentieth century, the Presbyterian Church owned large tracts of land on the northern edge of downtown Santa Fe and a good deal of it was dedicated to schools for rural New Mexican children. In 1908, the Presbyterians built the Mary James Missionary Boarding School for Boys just west of where the Masonic Temple stands today. It was named for a leading missionary and the first president of the Women's Board of Home Missions. But it closed five years later and boys of high-school age were sent to board at the Presbyterian-run Menaul School in Albuquerque.

The Mary James facilities were immediately taken over by the Allison School for Girls, an institution the church had been operating in a building on Grant Avenue just north of the First Presbyterian Church (see pages 50-51). The combined campus was renamed the Allison-James School, and in 1925, the Presbyterians dedicated the new Sage Memorial administration building. By 1934, the Allison-James School became a coeducational junior high boarding school with students drawn in large part from the villages of northern New Mexico.

But by the late 1950s the Presbyterian Board of National Missions recognized that it was duplicating the efforts of the New Mexican public school system, so in 1959 the church closed the Allison-James School. The school's buildings then became the temporary home of the State Historical Library. By 1964, all remaining structures were razed (except for a 1930 dorm building that's now the law offices of White, Koch, Kelley, and McCarthy), and the land developed into Plaza del Monte, a study and conference center and retirement facility for Presbyterian ministers and missionaries.

Presbyterian Mission School
Santa Fe N.M.

Grant Avenue

The Presbyterians opened their first school shortly after the Reverend David McFarland came to Santa Fe in 1866 and held classes in his home, a two-room adobe on Palace Avenue. By the time Matilda Allison arrived in Santa Fe in 1881 to take charge, classes were meeting in an old, rambling adobe that could barely keep out the rain. Eight years later she moved her school, then called the Santa Fe Industrial and Boarding School for Mexican Girls, into a new, three-story brick building on Grant Avenue just north of the First Presbyterian Church. Tuition was free and so were books for those who could not afford them. Those with means paid with whatever they had, including in one case "8 strings of chile, 1 sack of cornmeal, 1 sack of onions, $15 worth of wool, 1 Navajo blanket, 5 chickens, 1 box of grapes, and 2 dozen eggs." Miss Allison retired in 1903, whereupon the well-established school was renamed in her honor.

In 1927, the church sold this property to the Santa Fe Public Schools, which built Leah Harvey Junior High School, named for Santa Fe's first female insurance agent, on the site. That school was closed in the mid-1970s and the building remodeled into what is now the First Judicial District Court.

Presbyterian Mission School
(Allison-James School), ca. 1885.
Photo by Dana B. Chase.
(MNM # 110511)

17. First Presbyterian Church

208 Grant Avenue

The Baptists came to Santa Fe in 1849 as the first Protestants to try to organize a congregation in the heavily Catholic town. But they soon concluded that their work here was hopeless, and they left. The Presbyterians arrived shortly after the Civil War and, under the direction of the Reverend David McFarland, held their first services in the Palace of the Governors. In 1869 they bought and restored the ruins of an adobe church, which the Baptists had built and abandoned twenty years earlier at the intersection of Grant Avenue and Griffin Street. They used it until 1881. Among Reverend McFarland's many duties during his eight years in Santa Fe was to solemnize the common-law marriage of Catherine McCarty and William Antrim, Billy the Kid's mother and stepfather. Billy was a witness.

In 1881, the Presbyterians built a new brick church of midwestern formality behind the original adobe church. That was replaced in 1939 by a Spanish Pueblo Revival-style church designed by John Gaw Meem. Flanking its main entrance is a pair of massive buttresses that appear to have inspired those that wound up on the front of the San Miguel Mission Church after its remodeling in 1955 (see page 147).

Presbyterian Church, ca. 1880.
Photo by Ben Wittick.
(MNM # 15855)

Presbyterian Church.
Photo by J. Weltmer.
(MNM # 15175)

First Presbyterian Church, ca. 1977. Photo by Arthur Taylor. (Detail of MNM # 111924)

18. Santa Fe High School Campus

Marcy Avenue at Lincoln Avenue

Once Fort Marcy ceased operations in 1891, the block bordered by Marcy Avenue, Lincoln Avenue, Federal Place, and Grant Avenue went first to the City of Santa Fe before coming under the control of the Santa Fe Public Schools in 1904. The district then built the Catron School, designed by Isaac Hamilton Rapp and located near the northwest corner of Marcy and Lincoln (facing south toward Marcy Avenue). Until it was torn down in 1951, this building served all grades, from elementary through high school. In 1912, the school board took an old barracks building dating from the days of the fort, which ran north and south along Grant Avenue at the western edge of the property, and remodeled it into the Sena Building for use as a high school. This is where the Sweeney Convention Center now stands. In 1929, on land between these two buildings, the district built a third structure called Seth Auditorium, which housed a gymnasium and various classrooms.

In the early 1950s, all of this was removed and a new John Gaw Meem-designed Santa Fe High School and Sweeney Gym went up in its place. In 1977, the district built a new high school south of the city and the old building was converted into today's City Hall, while Sweeney Gym became the Sweeney Convention Center.

Catron School. (MNM # 9755)

Seth Auditorium, Santa Fe High School.
Photo by T. Harmon Parkhurst. (MNM # 147541)

Santa Fe High School, 1961. (MNM # 51955)

19. Centerline Building

207 Lincoln Avenue

Architect and interior designer John Conron, educated at Yale under the direction of Modernists Edward Durrell Stone and Louis Kahn, came to Santa Fe in 1952. He became an early and vocal critic of the faux adobe style then engulfing the city and the early efforts to codify it in city statute. His complaint was that this historic-style ordinance would do nothing to protect Santa Fe's historic buildings, and it would smother any architectural innovation. In 1954, he and his partner bought a circa-1910 brick cottage on Lincoln Avenue and remodeled it into a California Stick Modern Chalet to shelter their architecture practice and interior design shop. Despite lingering rumors that Conron set out to deliberately provoke those in favor of a historic design review and control ordinance, he insists his sole intent was to design and build the space he needed, in the contemporary style he preferred. Nevertheless, the shock of such an alien style in downtown Santa Fe served as a catalyst to speed the approval of the historic design ordinance. The city adopted it in 1957 and theoretically outlawed any future deviations from the Spanish Pueblo Revival and Territorial Revival styles. The Centerline Building lived on, however, and in 1979 it became home to The Soak, the city's first public hot tubs. But by 1985 The Soak was gone, the building was torn down shortly thereafter, and the site has been a parking lot ever since.

Centerline Building, July 1, 1979.
Photo by Arthur Taylor.
(Detail of MNM # 86460)

203 Lincoln Avenue

Santa Fe Sporting Goods had been operating at 109 1/2 Washington Avenue, near where the Burrito Company is today, since at least 1944. Sometime around 1950, it moved into a red-brick house at 203 Lincoln Avenue typical of the several nearby bungalows dating to around 1910. After 1960, Santa Fe Sporting Goods was gone, and for the next twenty years, this and the building next door at 201 Lincoln Avenue were home to a number of small retail shops under the name Lincoln Building. Eventually these two joined a number of other stores around the corner facing Marcy Avenue, got a brown plaster makeover, and the whole became the Lincoln Center Shopping Mall. In the early 1980s this complex slipped under the radar of the style police and underwent a very strange remodeling into what might be called Aztec Baroque that introduced details not seen anywhere else in the city.

Santa Fe Sporting Goods.
(Dale Bullock Photograph Collection,
Image No. 31051, New Mexico State
Records Center and Archives.)

21. Little Chief Grill Cafe/La Esquina Building

112 Marcy Avenue

West Marcy Avenue, ca. 1977.
Photo by Arthur Taylor.
(Detail of MNM # 112193)

Until the late 1970s, this once-proud Queen Anne-style house stood back from the corner of Lincoln and Marcy Avenues. Over time, in a classic case of commercial accretion, a series of single-story stuccoed commercial buildings filled in the space between the house and both streets. When this photograph was taken in 1977, two of the spaces facing Marcy Avenue were occupied by the Little Chief Grill Cafe and Durr's, a typewriter repair shop.

Around 1980, engineer Roger Bybee created a partnership with electrical contractor Otis Beaty to redevelop the property. They tore everything down and in their place built a five-story office building. The project sparked a cry of outrage among Santa Feans who saw how their beloved city was being overrun by faux adobe buildings standing far higher than they had any right to. Someone expressed this sentiment in hostile graffiti on the protective barricades at the construction site: "Courtesy of City Hall *pendejo vendidos*," which politely translates to "Courtesy of a bunch of stupid City Hall sellouts."

La Esquina Building under construction, February 1982. Photo by Richard Wilder. (MNM # 122817)

22. Montgomery Ward Order Office

125 Lincoln Avenue

When photographed in the mid-1950s, this row of commercial buildings along the east side of Lincoln Avenue near the corner of Marcy Avenue included the Montgomery Ward Order Office, the Maytag Shop, the Batrite Pastry Shop, and Batrite Food Stores. To the right of the alley was the Sebastian Firestone Dealer Store, which at one time had been a popular watering hole called Hazel Cash's Bar. But the whole row was torn down in the early 1980s, and in a massive, over-scaled development that extended through to Washington Avenue and out to Marcy Avenue, the four-story First Interstate Building went up in its place (see page 45).

Lincoln Avenue, ca. 1955.
Photo by Tyler Dingee.
(MNM # 91914)

117–119 Lincoln Avenue

The Rapp brothers designed this theater – identified on the 1913 insurance map as the Elks Opera House – for a site next door to the Elks Club, which their firm had designed two years earlier (see pages 66-67). The theater was torn down around 1940, replaced two years later by a building that housed the New Mexico Gas Tax Division, with Hazel Cash's Bar next door. Within a few years, J. L. Hair and Sons, dealers in auto accessories, took it over. From 1951 to 197c, the building was a Firestone tire dealership, after which it became home to Hill's Handcrafted Furniture. In 1973, Hill's began sharing the building with Los Caballeros Cafeteria. Both were gone by 1975, replaced by other small businesses, and two years later the site was cleared entirely. It has been a parking lot for Museum of New Mexico employees ever since and is soon to be the site of a new museum annex.

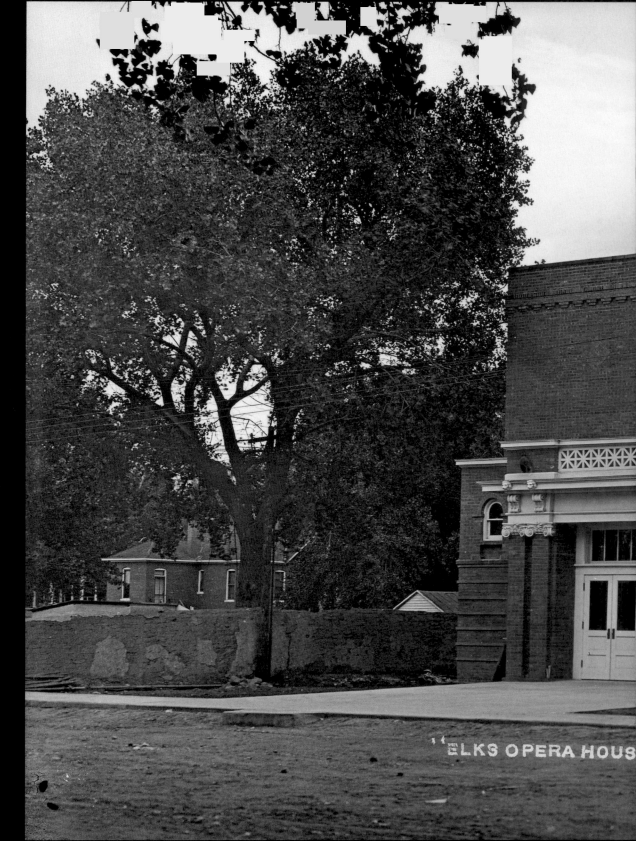

Elks Theater, 1909.
Photo by Jesse L. Nusbaum.
(MNM # 61368)

ANTA FE, NEW MEX.

24. Elks Club

111–113 Lincoln Avenue

As part of the 1904 St. Louis World's Fair celebrating the hundredth anniversary of the Louisiana Purchase, Rapp & Rapp designed a Mission Revival building that looked similar to this one to promote the New Mexico Territory. When the Santa Fe Elks Club hired the Rapp firm to build it a new headquarters in 1911, the brothers rolled out the St. Louis drawings and this was the result. A 1912 photograph shows a warm and comfortable interior of oak paneling, and a room furnished with Arts and Crafts tables and chairs and brass spittoon. Throughout the 1930s Santa Feans found momentary relief from the Great Depression by playing the club's numerous slot machines.

In the early 1940s, the Elks Club building lost its Mission Revival identity when it was plastered over and reduced to a lifeless block of brown stucco. After the Elks built a new club out on Old Pecos Trail in 1963, the old building became the property of the Museum of New Mexico. The museum has now cleared this site to make room for a major expansion.

Elks Club, 1912.
Photo by Jesse L. Nusbaum.
(MNM # 61366)

25. Fine Arts Museum

Lincoln Avenue at Palace Avenue

In the days of Fort Marcy, when the United States Army garrisoned troops in downtown Santa Fe and constituted one of the city's major sources of revenue, a building at the northwest corner of Lincoln and Palace Avenues served as its barracks and administrative headquarters. But by 1902, the army had left, its revenue stream had dried up, and the former fort's holdings had changed roles. One corner of the building, for instance, sheltered the city's library until it moved into a new home on Washington Avenue (see pages 38-39). After that, the deteriorating old fort headquarters became a billiard hall and private offices.

By 1909 a group of museum employees who believed that Santa Fe's economic future would be tied to making the city a center for Southwest

Copy of Rapp plan of Colorado Supply Company Store, Morley, Colorado, 1912. Photo by Jesse L. Nusbaum. (MNM # 61210)

Mission San Estevan, Acoma Pueblo, ca. 1935. Photo by T. Harmon Parkhurst. (MNM # 7864)

tourism began a four-year restoration of the Palace of the Governors. Their goal was to revive interest in Santa Fe's original vernacular architecture and to create a distinctive and homogeneous architectural character, especially for the downtown, that would replace the rash of different styles that had come with the railroad. They combed the city and the mission churches for examples of posts, beams, corbels, and other details that exemplified traditional adobe architecture, and they unveiled their findings on November 18, 1912, at a public exhibition called *New-Old Santa Fe.*

Included in their presentation were the original drawings the Rapp & Rapp architectural firm had produced for a warehouse in Morley, Colorado, that had been inspired by the San Estevan del Rey Mission Church at Acoma Pueblo. Two years later, this same design became the basis for the New Mexico building the Rapp brothers created for the 1915 Panama-California Exposition in San Diego.

By now the Palace of the Governors had outgrown its capacity to host art shows, and Rapp & Rapp was chosen to design a new Fine Arts Museum for the site of the old fort's headquarters. Seeing no need to reinvent the wheel, the brothers dusted off the Morley warehouse/San Diego plans for a building whose details would become the quintessence of the new Santa Fe style. In the

New Mexico Building, Panama-California Exposition, 1915, San Diego, California. Photo by Jesse L. Nusbaum. (MNM # 60256)

process, as Isaac Hamilton Rapp's biographer Carl D. Sheppard wrote, they "gave back to Santa Fe its Hispanic past." The twin-tower look flanking the museum's entrance, which emulated those on the church at Acoma Pueblo, went on to adorn several other important buildings in Santa Fe, including the west façade of La Fonda hotel (see page 19), El Oñate Theater (now the First National Bank; see page 85), and the federal building opposite St. Francis Cathedral (see pages 24-25).

Fine Arts Museum, ca. 1920. Photo by T. Harmon Parkhurst. (MNM # 22973)

26. Fort Marcy/Bishop Building

123 West Palace Avenue

Unidentified parade on West Palace Avenue. (MNM # 99587)

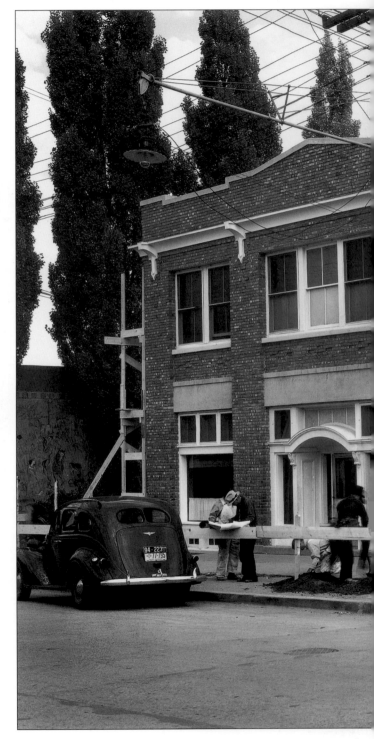

From the time the United States Army first occupied New Mexico in 1846, this stretch of West Palace Avenue was a part of Fort Marcy. The one-story building with a hipped roof may once have been the fort's bakery, but by 1898, according to an insurance map, it was a kindergarten. On the 1908 map it was identified as a defunct steam laundry.

By 1915, it had been replaced by a two-story building that served, until 1942, as the headquarters of *The Santa Fe New Mexican*, which had been founded in 1849 and remains "The West's Oldest Newspaper."

In the late 1930s the building got a Territorial makeover, and from 1943 to the end of World War II, the U.S. Army used it as a check-in point for the men and women who worked on the top-secret Manhattan Project in Los Alamos. For many years it has been known as the Bishop Building and today it is an art gallery.

Bishop Building,
November 11, 1955.
Photo by Gertrude Hill.
(MNM # 51861)

Santa Fe New Mexican, ca. 1935.
Photo by T. Harmon Parkhurst.
(MNM # 10725)

27. Evans Motor Company/Bokum Building

142 West Palace Avenue

For close to twenty years, people bought cars and tires in this building on West Palace Avenue at the corner of Burro Alley. When this photograph was taken in 1932, Evans Motor Company, a Dodge dealership, occupied the site, and the Nash Motor Company had been there before that. By 1940, the building was home to Emblem and Lawrence Autos, which two years later was known as Henry Lawrence Autos. Two years after that it became the Jimmie Austin Tire Company. For a few years in the early 1950s the building sheltered a variety of printing companies, and by 1957 it had been razed and replaced by the three-story Bokum Building that remains there to this day.

Evans Motor Co., ca. 1935.
Photo by T. Harmon Parkhurst.
(MNM # 10722)

Bokum Building, 1984. Photo by Richard Wilder. (Detail of MNM # 148045)

28. Courtyard Houses/Santa Fe County Courthouse

102 Grant Avenue

Until the late 1930s, this block of Grant Avenue was occupied by two adjoining adobe courtyard houses. The one to the south had once been the home of Gertrudis Barcelo, otherwise known as Doña Tules, Santa Fe's infamous madam and gambling maven. She was the best monte dealer in town, and in her "sporting emporium" hundreds of thousands of dollars changed hands. She controlled the city's vice in the middle years of the nineteenth century and is said to have amassed a handsome fortune in the process.

In the 1930s the house to the north was the law office of Jacob H. Crist, a defense attorney who became involved in a notorious murder case in 1931. Tom Johnson, a poor black man, was falsely accused of killing Angelina Jaramillo, the eighteen-year-old daughter of a well-connected local family, in her home just up the block on Griffin Street. Crist mounted a vigorous defense before Judge Miguel Otero in the 1909 county courthouse on East Palace Avenue (see page 29) but ultimately failed to save the life of Johnson, who was put to death in 1933 in the state's first electrocution. In *Justice Betrayed: A Double Killing in Old Santa Fe*, Ralph Melnick makes a convincing case that the real murderer was in fact a member of Angelina's own family and that his crime had been covered up by racism and political patronage.

In 1939, the block was cleared and a new John Gaw Meem-designed Santa Fe County Courthouse was built on the site under the auspices of the WPA. Meem embellished it with several authentic details, like the split-cedar ceiling over the *portal*, the punched-tin light fixtures, and the richly carved rope-spiral balusters on the interior staircase. While the entrance courtyard originally faced north onto Johnson Street, in 1974 an addition that now serves as the county assessor's office filled in the façade and the front door was moved to the Grant Avenue side.

Grant Avenue at Johnson Street. (MNM # 10668)

Santa Fe County Courthouse, July 24, 1979. Photo by Arthur Taylor. (MNM # 89017)

29. Palace of the Governors

North side of the Plaza

Don Pedro de Peralta arrived in 1610 to found *La Villa Real de Santa Fe de San Francisco de Asis* and laid out a town around a central plaza according to the Laws of the Indies. His primitive adobe-brick presidio, with towers at its four corners, enclosed the area that today is bounded by Palace Avenue, Washington Avenue, Lincoln Avenue, and South Federal Place. A row of rooms that flanked the northern edge of the town's Plaza have survived to become today's Palace of the Governors.

The history of this building, at least as related by J. K. Shishkin in a 1972 booklet called *The Palace of the Governors*, is a recitation of one corrupt governor after another, the persistent abuse they heaped upon their Native American slaves, and their repeated (and often failed) attempts to wrest some profit from the harsh landscape. On August 13, 1680, the Indians rose up in bloody revolt, drove the Spaniards south across the border into El Paso, and for the next dozen years occupied what remained of the burned-out Palace, which they converted into a four-unit communal dwelling. That is where Don Diego de Vargas Zapata Lujan Ponce de Leon found them when he and a small band of Spanish followers reoccupied Santa Fe on September 13, 1692.

The building has served as governmental headquarters for a succession of Spanish, Mexican, and finally American government officials. After the arrival of the U.S. Army in 1846, the Palace received a simple Territorial-style *portal* with Greek Revival detailing. In 1877, U.S. Marshal John Sherman added a plank sidewalk, wrapped the porch posts with elaborate moldings, and capped it all with a heavy, Victorian balustrade. Nevertheless, the Palace

Palace of the Governors, ca. 1867. Photo by Nicholas Brown. (MNM # 58758)

Palace of the Governors, ca. 1884. Photo by F. E. Evans. (MNM # 67223)

fell into increasing decrepitude. General Lew
Wallace, novelist and author of the timeless line
"Every calculation based on experience elsewhere
fails in New Mexico," finished *Ben Hur* in the
Palace while serving as Territorial governor from
1878 to 1881. In a request for $30,000 for long-overdue
renovations, he reported to Congress that "The
walls were grimy, the undressed boards of the floor
rested upon the ground, the cedar rafters, rain-
stained as those of the dining hall of Cedric the
Saxon, and overweighted by tons and tons of mud
composing the roof, had the threatening downward
curvature of a shipmate's cutlass." He was refused.

A proper state capitol building was built south
of the Santa Fe River in 1886, but a mysterious fire
consumed it just six years later, forcing government
officials temporarily back into the old Palace. Once
a new capitol building opened 1900, the Palace was
used for several years as private offices.

In 1909, the Palace became the property of the
School of American Archaeology and underwent a
four-year reconstruction. Museum officials replaced
the Victorian *portal* with a Spanish Pueblo Revival
one in an attempt to return the building to the
way they believed it may have looked in the
eighteenth century. In the process, they set in
motion the effort to establish a new Santa Fe style
based on the traditional elements they gleaned from
older Santa Fe structures and mission churches (see
pages 68-71). They then used this homogeneous
style to promote Santa Fe's unique architectural
history and establish the city as the locus of
Southwest tourism. Today the building serves as
the Museum of the Palace of the Governors.

Palace of the Governors. (MNM # 6720)

30. The Plaza

As a Spanish colonial city, Santa Fe was laid out at its founding in 1610 in accordance with the Laws of the Indies. These ordinances, promulgated by King Philip II of Spain in 1573 to control town planning throughout the New World, called for a plaza at the center of the town. With a length ideally one and a half times its width (a shape well suited for fiestas and horse-mounted drills), the plaza would be framed by buildings fronted by *portales* to protect citizens from rain and sun and to give them a place to gather and trade. The most important site was chosen for the church, which sat upon the high ground at the eastern edge where the Cathedral is today (see page 23). The government buildings were arrayed along the Plaza's northern edge (see pages 78-79). And the other two sides were reserved for the homes of prominent citizens and for commerce.

Santa Fe's layout met these requirements, and into the middle of the nineteenth century citizens held their market at the west end of the Palace of the Governors and under trees in the Plaza. Trade activity picked up considerably in the years of the Santa Fe Trail (1821-80) as wagoneers from Missouri used the open space to display and sell their wares. A bandstand that stood in the center of the Plaza (visible in early photographs) was moved to the northern edge in 1868 to make way for a new monument to the heroes of the Civil War. At its base is an inscription that also acknowledges (reflecting the prejudices of the times) the sacrifice of those who fought the "savage" Indians. One day in the 1970s, a man dressed in

Plaza, ca. 1868-69. (MNM # 11252)

overalls quietly climbed over the wrought-iron fence around the monument, opened a bag of tools, took out a hammer and chisel, obliterated the word "savage," packed up his tools, and left. Who he was remains a mystery, but the effect of his chiseling endures.

After the coming of the railroad in the 1880s, the adobe commercial and residential buildings around the Plaza were replaced by larger, Victorian designs. These buildings were fashioned of brick and embellished with imported manufactured architectural details. As New Mexico approached statehood, tastes changed again. Many of the Italianate commercial blocks were remodeled to conform to the Spanish Pueblo Revival and

Territorial Revival styles, and most were stripped of their Victorian finery and either plastered or painted various shades of brown.

By the 1970s, many local anchors, like the high school, the hospital, and major retail stores, had left the downtown core, and the sixty-year effort to remake Santa Fe into a center for tourism was virtually complete. Once a shady spot for residents to meet and visit, today the Plaza is mostly devoid of local Santa Feans, who seldom find a reason to go downtown. Now tourists occupy the benches and the Plaza fills for the annual Fiesta, Indian and Spanish Markets, and a host of other celebrations, including craft shows, speeches by visiting dignitaries, and protests.

Plaza, ca. 1912. Photo by Jesse L. Nusbaum. (Detail of MNM # 139151)

31. Capital Hotel/El Oñate Theater

Lincoln Avenue at Palace Avenue

Gustave Elsberg and Jacob Amberg, cousins of German-Jewish descent who were involved with trade on the Santa Fe Trail, put up a two-story commercial building with a *portal* and second-story porch on the northwest corner of the Plaza in 1863. *The Santa Fe New Mexican* hailed it as "the most commodious and elegant building in New Mexico." It had twenty-six rooms, with stores on the ground floor and meeting rooms for the Masons and Odd Fellows upstairs. By 1884, the building had become the Capital Hotel. From 1898 to about 1913 it was the home of *The New Mexican* until the paper moved into its new headquarters at the corner of West Palace Avenue and Sheridan Street (see pages 72-73).

The building remained essentially physically unchanged into the early years of the twentieth century. Eventually, ownership fell to J. B. Lamy, nephew of Archbishop Jean Baptiste Lamy, who removed the Territorial portal and porch. It was then occupied by the Monarch Cash Grocery until a gas explosion in December 1917 destroyed the front of the building.

Following a liquidation sale, the building was razed and the lot stood empty for several years. In 1921, J. C. Cassell Jr. opened El Oñate Theater, one of Santa Fe's early motion-picture houses. It was built in the new Spanish Pueblo Revival style with a pair of towers that mimicked those at the Acoma mission, the same element that had appeared in the design for the Fine Arts Museum across the street (see page 71). Its lobby was decorated with two dramatic murals by

Capital Hotel, ca. 1884. Photo by J. R. Riddle. (MNM # 56237)

Palace Avenue at Lincoln Avenue, ca. 1919. (MNM # 57618)

*El Oñate Theater
(Cassell Building), 1921.
(Detail of MNM # 10661)*

famed local painter Gerald Cassidy, which today hang in the main post office on South Federal Place. The corner of the building, which originally served as Cassell's Nash and Jordan motor car dealership, was later opened up and during the 1930s and 1940s it operated as a drive-through service station and Dodge-Plymouth dealership. The movie theater closed in 1924 and part of the building was taken over by a dress shop. In 1953-54, John Gaw Meem remodeled the building into the headquarters of the First National Bank.

32. Claire Hotel/Ore House Restaurant

50 Lincoln Avenue

The Claire Hotel building, ca. 1916-17. (Detail of MNM # 10671)

In March 1892, Denver entrepreneur E. T. Webber opened the three-story Claire Hotel he had built on the west side of the Plaza. For many years he advertised it as the only fireproof and steam-heated hotel in the city. The pressed-brick and red sandstone structure, which had cost $75,000 to build, had twenty-six single rooms, hot and cold running water, and a passenger elevator. It was said to be the best equipped in New Mexico.

Julius Gans bought the building in 1929, and for years it housed a series of small businesses and professional offices. During World War II the city fire inspector cited the structure, then known as the Renehan Building, for wiring deficiencies, but a wartime shortage of materials delayed any improvements. Time ran out on September 5, 1946, when a fire destroyed the once fireproof building. Gans rebuilt the Renehan Building as a John Gaw Meem-designed, two-story, Territorial-style structure and called it the Plaza Building. But fire struck again on April 8, 1976, two years after Julius Gans's son Harold had sold it to Armand Ortega, a jeweler from Arizona. Rebuilt again, the building still houses Ortega's jewelry store and a women's clothing store named Mimosa at ground level, while the Ore House Restaurant has occupied the second floor since 1977. Visible in the original photograph on the right-hand corner of the hotel building is a pilaster with a Corinthian capital, one of four that once graced the ground-floor front. If you look carefully today, against the wall between the Plaza Restaurant and the shop to the left, it's still there, now painted Santa Fe brown, a lingering remnant of the old hotel.

Ore House on the Plaza, 2003. Photo by Bonita Barlow.

33. South Side of the Plaza

East San Francisco Street

After Mexico won its independence from Spain in 1821, New Mexico became the northernmost province of the new Republic of Mexico. The most immediate and visible change was the shift in attitude surrounding trade with the United States. The Spanish had barred American merchants from the area, but now Mexican officials in Santa Fe welcomed the foreign adventurers who gladly made the 800-mile trek from the Missouri River to trade pots, pans, and calico cloth for silver and furs.

These early traders parked their wagons in what was then a treeless, hard-packed, and dusty Plaza, spread out a dazzling array of goods, and soon turned this stretch of East San Francisco

Santa Fe Trail wagon trains, ca. 1869-71. Photo by Nicholas Brown. (MNM # 70437)

San Francisco Street at Plaza, 1950.
Photo by Tyler Dingee. (MNM # 91918)

San Francisco Street, 1965.
Photo by Karl Kernberger. (Detail of MNM # 43378)

Street into the city's commercial center. By the early 1870s the Plaza had been enclosed with a fence, yet the buildings opposite retained their rustic, single-story simplicity.

The one exception was a two-story structure owned by merchant Simon Delgado. It stood on the site of a former Spanish military chapel known as La Castrense that dated from 1760. With the shift of power from Spain to Mexico, the chapel had fallen into disrepair and closed in 1835. After the arrival of the American army in 1846, it became an ammunition storeroom and then a courtroom.

Responding to local indignation, Bishop Lamy restored it and used it as a chapel until 1858, when he sold it to Delgado for $2,000 in cash and some land near San Miguel Chapel. Lamy used the money to repair La Parroquia (see page 22) and the land for St. Michael's College (see pages 148-153). The next year, to help raise money for his cathedral, Lamy sold additional land east of the former chapel site to merchant Levi Spiegelberg, who with his four brothers had become fast friends of the prelate.

In the 1880s, after the arrival of the railroad, the old Spanish *portales* were removed and new buildings around the Plaza went up in the Victorian Italianate style. The Spiegelberg brothers built two stores on their land, one an elaborate wholesale and retail store (with raised pediment, projecting cornice, decorative brackets, and heavy eyebrowed windows) where upstairs tenants included the Masonic Hall and the Second National Bank, and a second, less imposing structure next door.

By 1950, most of the block – except for the larger Spiegelberg building – had been stripped of its Victorian details and looked like Main Street in any midwestern town, with a mix of cafes, hotels, and retail shops for locals. In an extensive renovation that began in the 1960s, most of the remaining elements of the railroad-era architecture were removed and the buildings encased in brown cement plaster in keeping with the "pueblofication" of Santa Fe.

By 1967, the entire Plaza was ringed by *portales*, something John Gaw Meem had proposed more than thirty-five years before, and within slightly more than a decade most stores catering to local needs were replaced by tourist-oriented businesses.

34. Beacham-Mignardot Hardware Co./J.C. Penney Co.

50 East San Francisco Street

According to the 1915 business directory, William Beacham and George Mignardot were already in the hardware and furniture business on the east side of the Plaza. Soon thereafter they moved to the corner of San Francisco Street and Don Gaspar Avenue. By the time this photograph was taken in 1934, the Beacham-Mignardot Hardware Company was announcing a "Quitting Business" sale with dishes selling for one-third off.

J. C. Penney soon took over the building and gave it a handsome Spanish Pueblo Revival makeover. In the mid-1950s, Penney's moved a few doors up the street to a location directly across from the Plaza (see page 89). Subsequently given a more Territorial Revival look, many different retail businesses have occupied this building since.

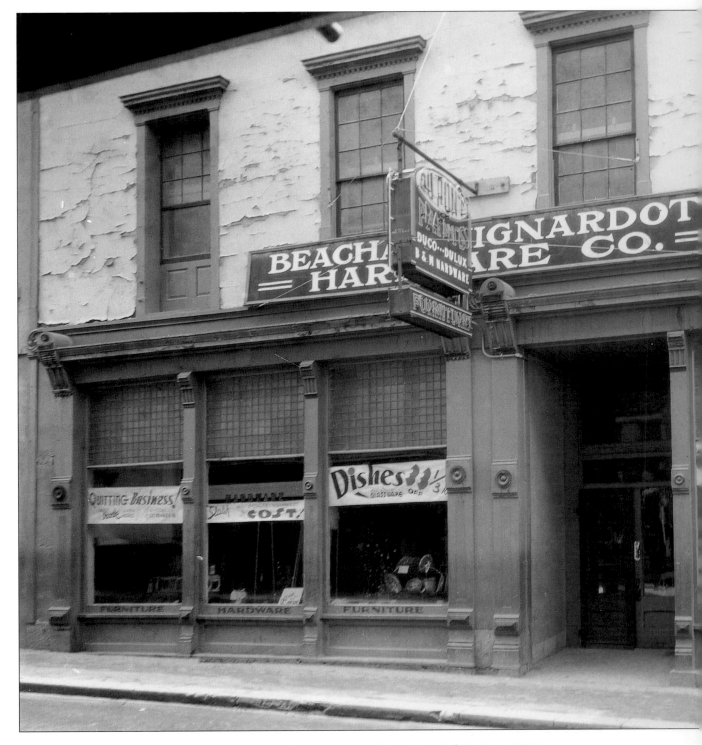

Hardware store, ca. 1935. Photo by T. Harmon Parkhurst. (Detail of MNM # 10723)

J. C. Penney Company. Photo by Fred K. Thompson. (Courtesy of Virginia Thompson)

35. Commercial Hotel/Central Pharmacy/Spirit & Corsini

107–109 West San Francisco Street

The First National Bank, founded in 1870, occupied the ground floor of this building from the time it was built in 1882 until 1912, when the bank moved into its grand new Rapp & Rapp-designed Greek Revival headquarters on the east side of the Plaza (see page 34). A telegraph office then took over the old space. Five years later it was home to the Commercial Hotel. On the day this photograph was taken a poster in a street-level window advertised the Charlie Chaplin film *Rink*, which had been released in 1916.

By 1956 the building had been shorn of its Victorian arched cornice and eyebrowed windows and its last tenant, Central Pharmacy, had moved on. Now it was boarded up and ready for demolition. The next year it was torn down and replaced by a one-story building leased by Shaya's Jewelry, which remained there for almost twenty-five years. When the jewelry store moved into the new First Interstate Bank building on Washington Avenue in 1982, a shop called Spirit took over the space. Spirit now shares the building with Corsini, another clothing boutique.

Commercial Hotel, ca. 1915-20.
Photo by T. Harmon Parkhurst.
(Detail of MNM # 14033)

Spirit and Corsini, 2003. Photo by Bonita Barlow.

Salmon Building, February 12, 1956.
Photo by Gertrude Hill.
(MNM # 51921)

36. The Big Dry Goods Store

111 West San Francisco Street

Wholesale and retail merchant Nathan Salmon built this two-story building to house The Big Dry Goods Store in 1906. Salmon, with his son-in-law E. John Greer, went on to build a real estate dynasty that still controls a great deal of property along West San Francisco Street. The dry goods store operated under various names – the last being the New Emporium – up until the late 1950s. Eventually the site was cleared of this and several other single-story Salmon/Greer-owned buildings to the west. It has served ever since as a parking lot for the First National Bank.

Nathan Salmon's The Big Dry Goods Store, 1912.
Photo by Jesse L. Nusbaum.
(MNM # 61442)

37. Laughlin Building

104 West San Francisco Street

In 1883, the corner of West San Francisco Street and Don Gaspar Avenue was the site of the National Hotel, which three years later disappeared from the insurance maps. In 1902, N. B. Laughlin – Civil War veteran and at various times lawyer, banker, judge, and dealer in mines who did all he could to avoid using his given name, Napoleon Bonaparte – bought some property there, a building described on that year's insurance map as a burned-out ruin. Laughlin then engaged the Rapp & Rapp architectural firm to design a commercial block, which he built in 1905. It housed his United States Bank and Trust Company until it went under in the depression of 1916. In later years, Laughlin's holdings would extend west along West San Francisco Street to Galisteo Street, as well as south along Don Gaspar to Water Street where the Montezuma Hotel occupied the corner (see pages 124-125).

When the camera captured this lovely lady strolling up West San Francisco Street around 1918, the city was undergoing a dramatic transformation from horse-drawn to motorized transportation. Today the second-story bay windows of the Laughlin Building are gone and the storefronts are shaded by a single-story *portal* that runs the length of the block. However, the iron post holding up the corner of the Laughlin Building that appears in this 1918 photograph is still there in front of the entrance to a store.

United States Bank and Trust Company, ca. 1905-1915. (MNM # 14031)

West San Francisco Street, ca. 1918. Photo by Wesley Bradfield. (MNM # 14142)

38. Paris Theater/ El Paseo Theater/ Teen World/ Banana Republic

123 West San Francisco Street

For more than half a century, the heart of Santa Fe's nightlife beat along West San Francisco Street where Nathan Salmon and his son-in-law, E. John Greer, controlled three movie theaters. Salmon's first entertainment venture was the Paris Theater, which appeared in the business directory in 1915. It was followed by the elaborate Moorish Revival Lensic Theater, built in 1930 at the corner of West San Francisco Street and Burro Alley. In ten years came the simpler Alley Theater (see page 107) across the street from the Lensic.

Throughout the 1930s, the Paris Theater specialized in cowboy-and-Indian films starring the likes of Tom Mix and Buck Jones, while the Lensic was reserved for first-run Hollywood features and the Alley showed Mexican movies. In the late 1940s, fire destroyed the Paris

*Paris Theater,
June 1945.
(MNM # 137065)*

El Paseo Theater, 1959. Photo by Tyler Dingee. (MNM # 91900)

El Paseo Theater Building, ca. 1976-1977. Photo by Arthur Taylor. (MNM # 117197)

Theater. It was rebuilt and reopened in 1951 as El Paseo Theater and remained in operation until 1972. For a short period it served as Teen World. The theater reopened in 1984 under the management of Bill and Judy Hill. At the time, they were operating the popular City Lights movie theater in the Pen Road Shopping Center, famous for its homemade refreshments. They rechristened their new movie palace El Paseo Theater and Café and introduced to Santa Fe the concept of viewing films while lounging on soft couches and built-in *bancos* or nibbling on snacks at tables and chairs arrayed along the walls. The theater closed for the last time in the early 1990s, after which the space was remodeled and leased to Banana Republic.

39. Z. Staab Building/Bell's Department Store

118 West San Francisco Street

Staab Building, C. Ilfeld Company, ca. 1935. Photo by T. Harmon Parkhurst. (Detail of MNM # 10778)

Brothers Zador and Abraham Staab, members of one of Santa Fe's leading German-Jewish merchant families, put up this building in 1884 shortly after the arrival of the railroad. By the time this photograph was taken in 1935, the Charles Ilfeld Co., which had been known as "Wholesalers of Everything" since 1865, had moved in.

Charles Ilfeld, head of another German-Jewish merchant clan with headquarters in Las Vegas, New Mexico, is fondly remembered for his generosity to a number of Lebanese immigrants who began moving into New Mexico around the time of statehood. One of them was Samuel Adelo, to whom Ilfeld provided – on credit – a wagon, a team of horses, and a wagonload of merchandise to peddle among the small villages and ranches within a sixty-mile radius of Las Vegas. Once he sold the goods, Adelo would return to Las Vegas, pay back his benefactor, reload, and set out again. Before long Adelo had opened his own store in Pecos, which survives to this day in the hands of his great-nephew. Up into the 1930s Adelo stocked his Pecos store by buying wholesale from the Ilfeld company at this Santa Fe location.

By 1938, Bell's Department Store took over the West San Francisco Street space. "Your Friendly Store" remained there into the early 1980s, when it and most of the other downtown stores that had served a local clientele either closed or moved into the new shopping malls well beyond downtown. The building was then demolished to make way for Plaza Mercado, a multistoried collection of tourist shops and restaurants.

Bell's Department Store, ca. 1977. Photo By Arthur Taylor. (MNM # 117310)

40. Taichert's Variety Store

120 West San Francisco Street

For many years this stretch of West San Francisco Street was the heart of downtown commercial Santa Fe, where locals shopped for shoes, clothing, groceries, and pharmacy needs. Taichert's was a five-and-dime variety store at the corner of Galisteo Street owned by Dan Taichert, a member of a German-Jewish family that had settled in Las Vegas, New Mexico, around the turn of the twentieth century. Taichert's moved two doors up the street in 1936, and from 1938 to 1969 the building was occupied by Kahn's Shoes. Within a little more than a decade, much of this block was replaced by Plaza Mercado, and the emphasis shifted from local to tourist shopping. But the building that originally housed Taichert's is still there.

Taichert's Variety Store, ca. 1935.
Photo by T. Harmon Parkhurst.
(MNM # 50965)

41. Herlow's Hotel/Alley Theater

212-216 West San Francisco Street

Since as early as 1882, when it first appeared in the business directory, Herlow's Hotel stood approximately opposite where the Lensic Theater is today. This photograph of the Corpus Christi procession heading up West San Francisco Street was taken sometime around 1886.

By 1930, this location was a dance hall and government supply warehouse. In 1940, Nathan Salmon and his son-in-law E. John Greer built the Burro Alley Theater (later known simply as the Alley Theater) on the site, their third movie house on the street (see pages 98-101), where local Santa Feans enjoyed Mexican films until 1968.

After the theater closed, the building was converted into the Bargain Center Furniture and Appliance Store. But by the start of the 1990s, most businesses on the street had changed from meeting local needs to those of tourists, and a jewelry shop took over this building. Today it has been divided into two stores that cater to the tourist trade.

Corpus Christi procession, ca. 1886. (MNM # 117450)

Burro Alley Theater. (Movie Stills Photographic Collection, New Mexico State Records Center and Archives, Image #41097)

42. Evans Hotel

230 West San Francisco Street

A brick-faced adobe building with arched second-story windows and a bracketed cornice appears to have been at this location as early as 1886, when its eastern corner was caught in the photograph of the Corpus Christi procession making its way up the street (see page 106). Between 1930 and 1933 it was the Alvarado Hotel. Sometime in the middle 1930s, when Pablo Duran had his real estate office next door, the building was known as the Evans Hotel, where you could get a meal at the Evans Cafe for a quarter and a haircut at the Alvarado Barber Shop. But the tenure of the Evans Hotel must have been brief, for that name never appears in a business directory. By 1936, the site was occupied by the Eagle Bar. That was followed in 1938 by the Reno Cafe. Eleven years later it was known as the Don José Bar, which remained into the 1960s. By 1968 the site was cleared. In the 1970s the city built a two-level parking lot, which in the 1980s became the three-level garage that's there today.

Evans Hotel, ca. 1929.
Photo by H. Sage Goodwin.
(MNM # 119354)

110 Sandoval Street

Montoya's Furniture and Hardware Co., 1950. Photo by Tyler Dingee. (MNM # 91912)

In the eighteenth century, the Antonio José Ortiz hacienda covered most of the block where the Hilton Hotel now sits. In 1855, the site became the property of Anastacio Sandoval, who gave his name to the street that runs along the property's eastern edge. He was a prominent merchant, soldier, and politician, and the site became the headquarters for his mercantile operations.

In 1945, after working through the Great Depression and the years of World War II in furniture stores owned by others, Robert R. Montoya and his father built their own furniture and hardware store on the former hacienda property near the corner of Sandoval and West San Francisco Streets. But in 1970 a large-scale urban renewal project forced them to move out of the downtown area. The site was cleared in 1972, the whole block developed into the Hilton Hotel, and the stretch of West Water Street that once continued to Jefferson Street (now Guadalupe Street) was closed for the hotel's parking lot. All that remains of the original hacienda today is a row of rooms along West San Francisco Street opposite the Eldorado Hotel.

Hilton Hotel, 2003. Photo by Kingsley Hammett.

44. Points Drive-In

212 Agua Fria Street

Points Drive-In. (Detail of MNM # 29171)

In the 1960s and 1970s, a massive urban renewal project radically changed the landscape and street pattern of the southwestern fringe of Santa Fe's downtown. Before then Agua Fria Street continued (from where it ends today at the Santuario de Guadalupe) diagonally across the Santa Fe River to terminate where today Water Street meets with Sandoval Street. Sitting on an irregularly shaped piece of land near the corner of Sandoval and West Alameda, in what today is the Hilton Hotel parking lot, was a popular liquor store called Points Drive-In, otherwise known as Five Points. It was owned and operated by Joe J. Hernandez and his family, who had owned the land for many years. Urban renewal buried many businesses on this site besides Point Drive-In, including the Pasatiempo Bar, Souders Supply Company, Tiny's Bar and Lounge, Vigil Brothers Bar, and the Santa Fe Electric Laundry. After the site was cleared, the streets were straightened and renamed, the Hilton Hotel was built on most of the land, and First National Bank put a drive-up branch on the former Points Drive-In location (see page 111).

Santa Fe Electric Laundry, ca. 1935. Photo by T. Harmon Parkhurst. (MNM # 54385)

45. Santa Fe County Jail

212 Water Street

The insurance map of 1883 indicates that this was the site of the city's offices. According to the 1898 map, this was also the location of the police court. In 1906, Santa Fe County engaged Isaac Hamilton Rapp to design a new jail to be built on the site as a fortress of dressed stone. On one side he placed an impregnable-looking jail with corners topped with octagonal towers. On the other he put a peaceful-looking cottage with a peaked roof that served as the sheriff's quarters. Rapp's interior layout made it possible for a single jailer to both hold off an escape from within and frustrate any attempt by an angry mob to break in from the outside. It was the city's first jail with lavatories for prisoners, *The New Mexican* reported upon its opening, and all new inmates were "given a bath whether they needed it or not."

The jail remained in this location until at least 1928 before moving into the brick building it shared with city offices and the fire department on Washington Avenue at the corner of East Marcy Avenue (where the city library now stands). The Water Street jail was then torn down and the space was used as a parking lot for El Fidel Hotel (see pages 116-117).

Santa Fe County Jail.
(MNM # 10248)

El Fidel Hotel

202-206 Galisteo Street

Joseph N. Fidel arrived in Northern New Mexico from his native Lebanon in 1910 and took up work as a traveling salesman between Las Vegas and Santa Fe. His brothers John, Philip, and Toufy soon followed, and by 1920 they were operating the Santa Fe Hay and Grain Company on Galisteo Street. In 1923, the brothers built El Fidel Hotel farther south on the next block of Galisteo Street, before building and operating two additional hotels – also named El Fidel – in Las Vegas and Albuquerque. The Santa Fe El Fidel was known as a commercial hotel, catering mostly to traveling salesmen, and was popular at a time when the only other quality lodgings in the city were at La Fonda (see pages 16-19) and the DeVargas Hotel (see pages 128-129). Many decades later, Joseph's son Michel could still remember stories of guests who checked in and requested rear-facing rooms on the upper floors so they could watch the hangings in the yard of the jail out back (see pages 114-115). In 1973, the hotel closed and was extensively remodeled by the First Northern Savings and Loan Association. Today there are retail shops at street level and the Otra Vez vacation condominiums above.

El Fidel Hotel, 1932.
Photo by T. Harmon Parkhurst.
(MNM # 50971)

47. Motley's Opera House

Galisteo Street

A business called the H. B. Motley Concert Hall, located on the east side of Galisteo Street, first appeared in the 1882-83 edition of *McKenney's Business Directory*. The 1889 edition called it a "saloon opera," and between 1909 and 1914 there are numerous references in various business directories to the "H. B. Motley restaurant." In the early days of motion pictures the opera house was converted into a movie theater.

Apparently the Motley family enterprises extended through to Ortiz Street, where Mrs. Motley is said to have run a rooming house (see pages 122-123). By the publication of the 1913 insurance map, the opera house had become a garage, and according to the 1921 map the site had been cleared altogether. Today this side of Galisteo Street is a string of shops in the Territorial Revival style catering to tourists.

Motley's Opera House.
Photo by Anna L. Hase.
(Detail of MNM # 16510)

48. Union Bus Depot/Water Street Plaza

126 West Water Street

From 1931 until 1984, interstate buses rolled into Santa Fe and came to a stop at the Union Bus Depot on Water Street, where new arrivals could find any number of moderately priced hotels and restaurants within a few blocks. By the mid-1980s, bus travel had declined in favor of private cars, Santa Fe had become an expensive tourist destination, and services for bus travelers had disappeared from the downtown area. The bus terminal relocated to a lonely and isolated stand-alone building south of town on St. Michael's Drive, far removed from hotels, restaurants, and other transportation. The old bus depot was then remodeled into the Water Street Plaza, and the nationally recognized restaurateur Mark Miller opened the Coyote Café and Coyote Cantina on the second floor.

Union Bus Depot. Photo by T. Harmon Parkhurst. (MNM # 51111)

Water Street Plaza, 2003. Photo by Bonita Barlow.

49. Ortiz Street

Between Water Street and Alameda Street

When this photograph was taken sometime between 1915 and 1920, a young woman stood in front of what could have been Mrs. Motley's rooming house while burros grazed along the ditch. Within a few years the back of the new DeVargas Hotel would loom above the narrow street and the burros would be replaced by cars. Today the street still is the back of things, including the Inn of the Governors on one side, and the Coyote Café and the shops fronting Galisteo Street on the other.

Ortiz Street, ca. 1915-20.
Photo by T. Harmon Parkhurst.
(Detail of MNM # 144777)

50. Normandie Hotel/Montezuma Hotel/Doodlet's

120 Don Gaspar Avenue

Prior to 1883, a one-story building known as the National Hotel sat on this corner. A second story was added sometime between 1902 and 1908, by which time the insurance map shows that this site was occupied by the Normandie Hotel. Its rooms cost between 50 cents and $1.50, and meals were available for 35 cents. When this photograph was taken in 1905, it captured what was reported to be the first automobile ever seen in Santa Fe, the car of some intrepid travelers stopping on their way to California. However, Nathan Salmon may actually have become Santa Fe's first motorist when he brought a Stevens-Duran into the city about that time.

By 1912, half a dozen years after putting up the Laughlin Building at the corner of Don Gaspar and West San Francisco Street (see pages 96-97), N. B. Laughlin completed his development of the west side of Don Gaspar Avenue. He took over the Normandie Hotel and renamed it the Montezuma Hotel. It catered to traveling businessmen – there was a telephone in every room – and business was so good that Laughlin soon added a third floor of rooms (note the shadow line that marks the transition from adobe to frame construction). The hotel remained in business through 1966, by which time it had earned the right to add the word "Historic" to its name. But by then the neighborhood had become quite run-down and most of the hotel's last guests were visiting opera singers in search of cheap lodgings whose warbling could be heard from the street below.

In 1967 Theodora Raven bought the building and opened a gift shop on the ground floor called Doodlet's, which remains to this day. Shortly after

The first automobile in Santa Fe, 1905.
(MNM # 11710)

she opened the shop, a drunken man with a woman on his arm walked in the door and asked for a room. When Theo told him the building was no longer a hotel, he replied, "That's all right; I only need it for half an hour."

Montezuma Hotel, ca. 1900-1910.
(MNM # 14034)

Doodlet's, 2003.
Photo by Kingsley Hammett.

51. Santa Fe Water and Light Company/
New Mexico Light and Power Company

201-204 Don Gaspar Avenue

For many decades the corner of Water Street and Don Gaspar Avenue was dominated by the city's power plant, whose twin stacks towered over the landscape. In 1880, the year the railroad arrived, *The New Mexican* announced with the gushing headline "Gas Begosh! Let Your Lights Shine Before Men" that the city now had its first great civic improvement – twenty-five gas street lamps. Within two years, budgetary considerations cut that number to four lamps, all around the Plaza. But in 1891 Santa Feans thronged the streets to see an even greater improvement as the switch was thrown at the plant that would now supply electric power to light the city's 320 lamps.

By 1925, Isaac Hamilton Rapp had designed a row of adobe-like offices fronting Don Gaspar Avenue where customers came to pay their utility bills. The plant and related buildings were gone by 1960 and the site has been used since as a city parking lot.

Santa Fe Water and Light Company, 1912. Photo by Jesse L. Nusbaum. (MNM # 61432)

New Mexico Light and Power Company. (MNM # 54394)

52. DeVargas Hotel

210 Don Gaspar Avenue

The DeVargas Hotel was built in 1923 in the Mission Revival style then in vogue in California. For many years is was a popular hostelry bustling with both local New Mexicans and visiting politicians, who socialized in the bar off the lobby and made deals upstairs in proverbial smoke-filled rooms. By the early 1980s the DeVargas had slid downscale into a rather seedy residence hotel. In 1986, it was remodeled into the more fashionable Hotel St. Francis that serves high tea in the lobby every afternoon.

Hotel DeVargas.
(MNM # 51371)

53. St. John's Methodist Church

216-218 Don Gaspar Avenue

In 1880 and for twenty years thereafter, St. John's Methodist Church occupied a steepled adobe building on West San Francisco Street. In 1901, the congregation laid the cornerstone for a new church on Don Gaspar Avenue, but the building remained unfinished until 1906. The Methodists left this site in the mid-1950s after they built a new, larger church south of downtown on Old Pecos Trail at the corner of Cordova Road. By 1960, this site had been cleared and has been used since as a parking lot for the DeVargas Hotel (now the Hotel St. Francis; see pages 128-129).

St. John's Methodist Church, May 1900.
Photo by Reverend John C. Gullette.
(Detail of MNM # 13256)

St. John's Methodist Church, February 13, 1956. Photo by Gertrude Hill. (MNM #70436)

54. Don Gaspar Avenue

Until the first decade of the twentieth century, vast areas of what is now prime real estate along West San Francisco Street, Water Street, and Don Gaspar Avenue were devoted to horse-transportation businesses – livery stables, carriage and harness repair shops, and feed and grain stores. But within a few years the city made a rapid transition to the automobile, and the same sites became car dealerships, parking garages, filling stations, and car repair shops. A leader in this transition was Charles Closson, who opened a livery stable in 1903 at the corner of Don Gaspar Avenue and East Alameda Street. Perhaps sensing the coming of the automobile, he and his son then built a garage down the street near where the parking lot of the Hotel St. Francis sits today.

By 1915, the Clossons got into car sales themselves, opening a Studebaker dealership at a time when only two other automotive enterprises were listed in the *New Mexico Business Directory*. When this photograph was taken in about 1928, Closson and Closson was selling Buicks. Over the next decades they dealt in various other makes, including Dodge, Marquette, Chevrolet, Cadillac, and LaSalle.

Across the street was Star Motors, which Harry Sauter and his partner Lowell Yerex opened in 1928. Yerex was a New Zealander who had been a flying ace for the British in World War I and

during the 1920s had barnstormed across West Texas and Eastern New Mexico. But their timing for the dealership was bad. The Great Depression soon forced its closure, and the pair wound up flying hops around Mexico and Central America, where Yerex founded TACA Airlines, whose successor is still the state airline of El Salvador. Sauter got caught in a Honduran revolution and was left for dead. Fortunately he survived, and a United Fruit Company banana boat evacuated him to a hospital in New Orleans. He eventually made his way back to Santa Fe and Don Gaspar Avenue, where he worked throughout the 1930s as a mechanic and top salesman for Closson Motors. In the 1940s, Sauter opened his own Pontiac dealership, which he sold in 1953 (see pages 154-155). By the late 1950s he was back in the car business, selling Studebakers for a short time from space he sublet from the Clossons. In 1965, he opened a Lincoln/Mercury dealership on St. Michael's Drive with his son Bill, to which they later added Toyotas.

The Clossons remained in business on Don Gaspar Avenue until at least 1955, after which the site of their dealership became known as Collins Lincoln Mercury (1957), Leonard Motors (1958), Hertz Rent A Car (1959), and various other small automotive businesses. By 1962, Thomas Closson Jr. leased the corner property to developers who built the Inn of the Governors, which remains today.

Don Gaspar Avenue. (MNM # 51490)

55. Quickel-Houk Motor Company/Santa Fe Village

227 Don Gaspar Avenue

Automotive enterprises dominated this side of the block of Don Gaspar Avenue across from the Closson family businesses for many decades in the middle of the twentieth century. Star Motors shared a row of four or five buildings with a succession of dealerships, including Emblem Motor Co. (1929), Wray L. Simmons Autos and the Driverless Car Rental (1930), Don Gaspar Motors (1938), Don Carlos Motors (1940), Withrow Motor Co. (1942), and Closson & Closson Used Cars (1957). The Quickel-Houk Ford dealership occupied this site from 1928 to at least 1933, and remained as Houk Motor Co. until at least 1936.

From 1944 until 1953, the building was the home of Saint Germaine Press, and for the next fifteen years it sheltered a few more auto dealerships and the headquarters of the state Motor Vehicle Division. In 1971, it was remodeled into the Santa Fe Village, a collection of small tourist shops. It looks like the work of an overeager Hollywood set designer: large patches of cement stucco are deliberately missing to reveal fake adobes, although the building is actually made of brick and hollow tile.

Quickel-Houk Motor Company. Photo by T. Harmon Parkhurst. (MNM # 54300)

Santa Fe Village, 2004. Photo by Kingsley Hammett.

56. Transcontinental Garage

Water Street at Old Santa Fe Trail

The intersection of Water Street and Old Santa Fe was dominated by automotive businesses for almost sixty-five years after the Transcontinental Garage, under the proprietorship of Olaf S. Emblem, first appeared in the *1913-1914 New Mexico Business Directory*. The shop was aptly named, for prior to 1937 – when a new, more direct route was carved across the middle of the state – motorists traveling from Chicago to Los Angeles on what would become the fabled transcontinental Route 66 swung northwest from Santa Rosa to Romero (later Romeroville) and followed the final fifty-eight miles of the old Santa Fe Trail into this very corner of the city. (They then headed south to Albuquerque before turning west toward Arizona.) Sometime around 1920 this corner became the city's Ford dealership and later a Texaco filling station (see pages 138-139).

Transcontinental Garage. (MNM # 184087)

Water Street at Old Santa Fe Trail

*Santa Fe Motor Company.
Photo by T. Harmon Parkhurst.
(MNM # 54265)*

When this photograph was taken in 1926, the corner had been home to Santa Fe Motors, the city's Ford dealership, since at least 1920. By the early 1930s the site had become Morris Motors and a Texaco gas station. Twenty years later it became a Chevron station, which it remained through the 1970s. But soon thereafter virtually all of Santa Fe's downtown filling stations – facing a more spread-out city, fewer motorists passing through downtown, and rising rents – left the area. These properties became galleries, gift shops, and branch banks. Today this site retains the original gas station building with its service bays and the portico where the pumps once stood, but it is used to sell jewelry and Latin American handicrafts to tourists.

Morris Motor Service, ca. 1935. Photo by T. Harmon Parkhurst. (MNM # 68815)

Water Street at Shelby Street

Thomas Motor Company, 1925. (MNM # 57815)

In 1925, when this photo reportedly was taken, the corner of Shelby and Water Streets was the home of Thomas Motor Company.

By 1940, Hunter Clarkson had moved his Indian Detours down the block from La Fonda hotel and was using this garage to park the large Packard touring coaches he used to take visitors on sight-seeing tours of surrounding pueblos. Nine years later, James I. Clarkson, Colonel Clarkson's brother, was operating Clarkson Motors, a Studebaker dealership, in this location. In 1955 Russ Hoswell took over the building and added a line of Packards to the Studebakers already available.

By 1972, the building had been converted into a mini-mall of tourist shops called El Centro, which remains today. The current structure retains the little belfry visible in earlier photographs.

Hoswell Motors, ca. 1955. (MNM # 91551)

El Centro, 2003. Photo by Kingsley Hammett.

59. Loretto Academy

Old Santa Fe Trail at Water Street

The Sisters of Loretto built this Second Empire-style structure in 1880 for their Loretto Academy, the school for girls they had founded in 1853 (see page 24). It was located just north of Loretto Chapel (famed for its Miraculous Staircase), the only remnant of the school's campus to survive. The miracle is that the chapel wasn't torn down (as originally planned) along with the rest of the complex after the school closed in 1968 and the land and structures sold to the developers of the Inn at Loretto. The Loretto Academy building was ultimately destroyed by fire and the site cleared. Nothing has taken its place but a parking lot associated with the hotel (see page 145) and a garden that has become an outdoor tourist market.

Loretto Academy and Chapel, May 1900.
Photo by Reverend John C. Gullette.
(Detail of MNM # 13262)

60. Loretto Convent/Inn at Loretto

211 Old Santa Fe Trail

Loretto Academy, May 1900. Photo by Reverend John C. Gullette. (Detail of MNM # 13262)

On this site south of the Loretto Chapel there once sat a hotel called La Casa Americana, the first two-story building in the city to have a pitched roof. From 1857 until 1892, it served as a convent for the Sisters of Loretto, after which the sisters built the imposing three-story structure pictured here. The sisters closed their girls' school in 1968 and in 1971 sold the four and a half acres and the convent, chapel, and academy buildings to the developers of the Inn at Loretto. During the 1973 demolition, a fire broke out in the convent that hastened its demise.

The 140-room steel-stud hotel, which opened in 1975, was built in a multistoried, stepped-back, Pueblo Revival design evocative of Taos Pueblo. Every Christmas its many tiers of parapets are trimmed with electric *farolitos* that mimic the votive candles Santa Feans traditionally set in bags of sand to symbolically light the path to the manger where the Christ child was born. They cast a warm glow over the hard plaster walls and make the Inn at Loretto one of the most photographed sites in Santa Fe.

Inn at Loretto, 2003.
Photo by Kingsley Hammett.

61. San Miguel Chapel

401 Old Santa Fe Trail

The original San Miguel Chapel was completed south of the Santa Fe River by 1626 for the Christianized Mexican-Indian servants who accompanied the early Spanish settlers and who lived separately in neighboring Barrio de Analco. After being destroyed during the Pueblo Revolt in 1680, it was rebuilt on the same site in 1710 with a three-tiered bell tower and adobe battlements.

San Miguel Chapel, May 1880. Photo by Ben Wittick. (MNM # 10110)

San Miguel Chapel, ca. 1891. (MNM # 49154)

When the Christian Brothers came to Santa Fe in 1859 to found St. Michael's College, a school for boys, they used the adobe chapel for daily worship. The deteriorated bell tower collapsed in a storm in the 1870s, and the louvered belfry, topped by a pitched roof that replaced it in 1887 gave the building a California Mission look. The ancient chapel was remodeled again in 1955, this time in the Spanish Pueblo Revival style.

San Miguel Chapel. (MNM # 29161)

62. Lamy Building

491 Old Santa Fe Trail

In 1878, Archbishop Lamy and the Christian Brothers erected the main building of St. Michael's College. At the time it was the tallest and largest adobe structure in the city, and its mansard roof, two-story porches, and central tower reflected Lamy's predilection for all things French. Classrooms and offices occupied the first two floors. The third was a dormitory for boarding students from around the state, who in the first decade of the twentieth century included a young man from San Antonio, New Mexico, named Conrad Hilton, of subsequent hotel fame. A major fire in 1926 destroyed the tower and third floor, which were never replaced, and the two remaining floors became dormitories. St. Michael's College (now the College of Santa Fe) left this location in 1947, after which the building served as a dormitory for St. Michael's High School (originally part of the college). In 1965, the brothers sold the building to the State of New Mexico, and today it houses several state offices.

San Miguel Chapel and St. Michael's School, 1881.
Photo by William. H. Jackson. (MNM # 1403)

Lew Wallace Building

495 Old Santa Fe Trail

Built in 1887 behind the San Miguel Chapel and the Lamy Building as part of the St. Michael's College campus, this building housed the school's kitchen and dining hall in the basement, a recreation room on the first floor, study halls on the second floor, and a storage attic on the top floor. In 1969, after the school had moved to new quarters south of town and the state had purchased the campus from the archdiocese, the building got a drastic remodel. Its pitched roof was removed and made flat and its front plastered to give it a Territorial Revival appearance. Today it holds the offices of *New Mexico Magazine.*

St. Michael's School, ca. 1924.
Photo by T. Harmon Parkhurst. (MNM # 51335)

64. Miguel Chavez Memorial Building

Old Santa Fe Trail near Paseo de Peralta

This building, dedicated in 1928, stood just south of the Lamy Building and held the classrooms of St. Michael's College. It was named for the philanthropist who pledged $25,000 for its construction. Chavez made several other significant donations to the local Catholic church, including funds for a building for the Sisters of Loretto (see page 144) and for the statue of Archbishop Lamy that stands before the Cathedral. In the 1960s the building was torn down and the Territorial Revival-style Public Employees Retirement Association building went up on the site, part of the state capitol complex that includes a circular, kiva-style statehouse, affectionately known as the "merry Roundhouse," across the street.

Miguel Chavez Memorial Building, ca. 1935.
Photo by T. Harmon Parkhurst. (MNM # 58004)

65. Harry Sauter's Storage Lot

Old Santa Fe Trail at Paseo de Peralta

From 1946 to 1953, Harry Sauter operated a Pontiac dealership at the northeast corner of Old Santa Fe Trail and Paseo de Peralta (where the parking lot of the PERA building sits today). Across the street, on the southeast corner, he had his storage lot, where in 1949 this phalanx of new Pontiac sedans was awaiting delivery to the Los Alamos National Laboratories.

In the early 1950s partners Free Fraser, Dick Kaune, and Sam Pate joined forces to build a small shopping strip on the site. It is still anchored at one end by Fraser Pharmacy ("Santa Fe's Oldest"), and at the other by Kaune Foodtown, the descendent of one of the city's longest continually operating businesses, which Henry Spencer Kaune founded on the Plaza in the middle 1890s.

1949 Pontiacs. (MNM # 148402)

Galisteo Street near East DeVargas Street

THE CAPITOL, SANTA FE.

Proposed Capitol design, ca. 1885. (MNM # 87442)

Territorial Capitol, ca. 1886-1888. Photo by J. R. Riddle. (MNM # 76041)

In 1852 the United States Congress authorized funds to start construction of a federal building that would have housed, among other functions, the Territorial legislature. But the flow of money was interrupted several times, and by the early 1880s only a single-story shell stood on South Federal Place at the north end of Lincoln Avenue. While it never did become the state capitol, it was eventually finished and today it serves as the federal courthouse.

In 1885, a wood engraving for a state capitol as grandiose as the Capitol in Washington, D.C., appeared on the front page of *The Santa Fe New Mexican*. It featured an enormous Classical center section topped by a tall dome and flanked by two wings, each with two additional domes.

The next year New Mexico finally got its first capitol, built just south of the Santa Fe River. Scaled to about one-third the size of the original design, which was never built, it had only two

domes. This building stood for just six years until a mysterious fire broke out in 1892.

After years of unsuccessful attempts to salvage both of the fire-damaged domes, Isaac Hamilton Rapp designed a new single-dome building with an imposing portico. Convict labor helped complete the project in 1900.

Following New Mexico's statehood in 1912, Santa Fe got caught up in the Spanish Pueblo Revival movement that was expressed in large

Capitol, ca. 1903. Photo by Christian G. Kaadt. (MNM # 10392)

public buildings like the Fine Arts Museum. But it took until the late 1920s and early '30s until John Gaw Meem began to incorporate Territorial details into the accepted Santa Fe look. He developed this new style from the simple Greek Revival detailing that the American army first introduced to Santa Fe in 1846. It included brick roof copings, square white columns with wood moldings to simulate bases and capitals, and white-framed windows topped with triangular pediments. The style soon found its way into many large local buildings.

In 1950, state architect Willard C. Kruger redesigned the capitol building. He stripped off the dome, portico, and all other Classical details; squared the windows; built a tower on the north façade; and covered the building with tan stucco topped with brick coping to give it a Territorial Revival appearance. However, some of its former Victorian elegance is still visible inside. Today the building is known as the Bataan Memorial Building, named for the many New Mexican servicemen who suffered and died in the Philippines during World War II, and it houses various state offices.

Bataan Memorial Building, 2003. Photo by Kingsley Hammett.

Agua Fria Street at Guadalupe Street

Few buildings in Santa Fe have been as "remuddled" as often or in as many differing styles as the Guadalupe Church, now known as the Santuario de Guadalupe. It was built in the late 1700s by Franciscans at the northern terminus of the *Camino Real*, the original trade route from Mexico. Its style was typical of eighteenth-century Mexican churches and it served its parishioners for almost 100 years.

In 1881, Archbishop Jean Baptiste Lamy directed fellow Frenchman Father James DeFouri to restore the badly deteriorated building. DeFouri demolished the original square tower, covered the flat roof with a steeply pitched shingled one topped by a tall steeple, framed the entryway with Italianate columns, cut Romanesque arched openings in the adobe walls, installed stained-glass windows, and added a white picket fence.

When a fire in 1922 destroyed most of the roof, the architectural inspiration shifted from rural France to the Spanish Mission Revival style then popular in California. The curvilinear parapets were coped with brick, the pitched roof clad in Spanish tile, and the steeple replaced by a square two-story bell tower with arched openings. In September 1941, the tracks of the Denver & Rio Grande railroad, which had run in front of the church since the 1880s, were torn up and sold as scrap. With the loss of the Chile Line, as it was called, Santa Fe was left as the only state capital without passenger rail service.

In 1961, the archdiocese built a new, larger, modern Guadalupe Church next door, and the old building was left to pigeons, vandals, and the

Wagon in front of Guadalupe Church, 1881. Photo by William H. Jackson. (MNM # 132561)

Guadalupe Church. (MNM # 10036)

Denver & Rio Grande Railroad, September 1, 1941, last narrow-gauge freight train. Photo by Margaret McKittrick. (MNM # 41833)

weather. Fifteen years later, in a particularly aggressive restoration of the original building, the brick copings were ripped off, the curvilinear parapets plastered straight, the Italianate columns flanking the front door and the Palladian window over it removed, and the Romanesque windows and the arches in the bell tower made square.

A final restoration in 1990 returned the brick-edged, undulating parapets and replaced the traditional mud plaster with cement stucco, leaving the church much as it had appeared in 1925.

*Santuario de Guadalupe,
ca. 1976.
(Courtesy Guadalupe Foundation)*

Santuario de Guadalupe, 2003. Photo by Jerilou Hammett.

Notes on Sources

The information for this book came from a variety of sources, including maps, business directories, books, newspapers, pamphlets, brochures, and interviews with individual Santa Feans. In some cases, facts, general information, and quotations from these sources are cited in the text. In other instances they have been gleaned from the sources described below.

Key to understanding the physical evolution of downtown Santa Fe is the information obtained through a close review of the Sanborn insurance maps available on microfilm at the New Mexico State Library, which were published by the Sanborn Map and Publishing Co. Limited, 11 Broadway, New York, New York, and cover the years 1883 to 1942. These maps are somewhat limited in their detail as far as identifying the uses of many particular buildings. Yet in other cases they offer a wealth of information, like the location of the gambling rooms in the Exchange Hotel/Capital Hotel. They also make clear the extent to which vast areas of what is now prime real estate were given over to livery stables, carriage- and harness-repair shops, and feed and grain stores until the early twentieth century. But within a decade of the appearance of the first automobile in Santa Fe in 1904 or 1905, many of those same sites were transformed into auto dealerships, parking garages, and car repair shops. By the 1930 map it is obvious that the conversion was complete and the downtown was dotted with new car showrooms, corner gas stations (said at one time to number twenty-seven), used car lots, and auto repair and paint shops.

Another key source of information was the many business directories available at the New Mexico State Library and the Fray Angelico Chavez History Library at the Museum of New Mexico. Volumes published between 1882 and 1927 cover several states in the Rocky Mountain region and thus only devote small sections to Santa Fe, while subsequent annual volumes cover Santa Fe exclusively. These directories, however, are not without their omissions and misspellings and at times appear to be slightly out of date. A business known to have one location might be listed at two different addresses at the same time, perhaps indicating it had moved between editions or was known to have plans to. And a company that went out of business in 1949, for example, might still be listed in the 1950 directory. Consequently, it was sometimes difficult to pinpoint exactly when a particular occupant was replaced by another, necessitating such qualifiers as "...the business remained in this location until at least 1936."

Several other books provided a variety of miscellaneous facts on some of Santa Fe's old buildings. These include *Santa Fe: A Pictorial History* by John Sherman (Norfolk: Donning Company, 1983) and *Old Santa Fe Today*. (Albuquerque: UNM Press for the Historic Santa Fe Foundation, 1991). The latter was particularly useful for its details on those buildings recognized as significant by the Historic Santa Fe Foundation, including La Castrense, the Catron Block, the Fort Marcy Officer's Residence, the Palace of the Governors, St. Francis Cathedral, St. Michael's Dormitory, San Miguel Chapel, and the Santuario de Guadalupe. Also helpful were *Santa Fe Then and Now* by Sheila Morand (Santa Fe: Sunstone Press, 1984); *Santa Fe: A Historical Walking Tour* by Jon Hunner, Shirley Lail, Pedro Dominguez, Darren Court, and Lucinda Silva (Chicago: Arcadia Publishing, 2000); *The Hospital at the End of the Santa Fe Trail* by Clark Kimball and Marcus J. Smith, M.D. (Santa Fe: Rydal Press, 1977); and *National Trust Guide—Santa Fe: America's Guide for Architecture and History Travelers* by Richard Harris (New York: John Wiley & Sons, Inc., 1997).

A number of histories of New Mexico and Santa Fe have been useful in providing information on both the city's architecture and its general evolution. These include *A Short History of Santa Fe* by Susan Hazen Hammond (San Francisco: Lexicos, 1988); *Santa Fe: A Modern History, 1880-1990* by Henry J. Tobias and Charles E. Woodhouse (Albuquerque: University of New Mexico Press, 2001); *The Last Conquistador: Juan de Oñate and the Settling of the Far Southwest* by Marc Simmons (Norman: University of Oklahoma Press, 1991); *The Far Southwest, 1846-1912: A Territorial History* by Howard R. Lamar (Albuquerque: University of New Mexico Press, Revised Edition 2000); and *The Santa Fe Trail* by R. L. Duffus (New York: David McKay Company, Inc., 1930, 1975). The work on which many of these histories is based is *Old Santa Fe: The Story of New Mexico's Ancient Capital* by Ralph Emerson Twitchell (Chicago: The Rio Grande Press), which is now out of print.

Two volumes of personal reflection lend color to the story of Santa Fe. The first is *Down the Santa Fe Trail and Into Mexico: The Diary of Susan Shelby Magoffin, 1846-1847* edited by Stella M. Drumm (Lincoln and London: University of Nebraska Press, 1926, 1962). The second, a collection of more contemporary reminiscences, is *Turn Left at the Sleeping Dog: Scripting the Santa Fe Legend, 1920-1955*, by John Pen LaFarge (Albuquerque: University of New Mexico Press, 2001).

Several books help flesh out the details behind specific buildings, including *Justice Betrayed: A Double Killing in Old Santa Fe* by Ralph Melnick (Albuquerque: University of New Mexico Press, 2002), which talks of the building once occupied by attorney Jacob Crist, where the Santa Fe County Courthouse now stands. Another is *Loretto: The Sisters and Their Santa Fe Chapel* by Mary J. Straw (Santa Fe: The Loretto Chapel Fund, 1984), which offers details on Archbishop Jean Baptiste Lamy, the

Sisters of Loretto, and the Loretto Chapel.

Details on the life and work of Isaac Hamilton Rapp are found in *Creator of Santa Fe Style: Isaac Hamilton Rapp, Architect*, by Carl D. Sheppard (Albuquerque: University of New Mexico Press, 1988). The life and work of architect John Gaw Meem are described in *John Gaw Meem: Pioneer in Historic Preservation* by Beatrice Chauvenet (Santa Fe: Historic Santa Fe Foundation/Museum of New Mexico Press, 1985) and two books by Chris Wilson – *The Myth of Santa Fe: Creating a Modern Regional Tradition* (Albuquerque: University of New Mexico Press, 1997) and *Facing Southwest: The Life and Houses of John Gaw Meem* (New York & London: W.W. Norton & Company, 2001). Personal interviews with Mr. Wilson also provided information about changes to the Coronado Building, the Fine Arts Museum, the Capital Hotel/First National Bank, the state capitol complex, the Santuario de Guadalupe, and other sites. This information first appeared in stories published in *DESIGNER/builder* magazine. Helpful descriptions of early Santa Fe town planning may be found in *The Architecture and Cultural Landscape of North Central New Mexico: Field Guide for the 12th*

Annual Vernacular Forum (held in Santa Fe, New Mexico, May 15-18, 1991), edited by Chris Wilson and Boyd C. Pratt.

Several facts and passages quoted from *The Santa Fe New Mexican* were obtained from microfilm files at the State History Library as well as from *Santa Fe: The Autobiography of a Southwestern Town*, edited by Oliver LaFarge (Norman, OK: University of Oklahoma Press, 1959).

Useful in tracing the changes that took place around the Plaza was the *Santa Fe Historic Neighborhood Study* written for the City of Santa Fe in 1988 by Beverly Spears and Corrine P. Sze. Many facts were confirmed by back issues of *El Palacio*, published by the Museum of New Mexico, and *La Herencia*, a quarterly magazine of Hispanic culture.

The history of the buildings associated with Santa Fe High School came from *Santa Fe High School, 1899-1999: Centennial History* by Marian Meyer.

Almost all of the historic photographs came from the Fray Angelico Chavez Photographic Archives of the Museum of New Mexico and are identified by their MNM negative number.

Flag Store and Star Restaurant, ca. 1900.
Photo by M.M. Salazar.
(MNM #35868)